SCIENCE ON THE INTERNET

A Resource for K–12 Teachers

Jazlin V. Ebenezer
University of Manitoba

Eddy Lau
University of Manitoba

Merrill
an imprint of Prentice Hall

Upper Saddle River, New Jersey   Columbus, Ohio

Library of Congress Cataloging-in-Publication Data
Ebenezer, Jazlin V.
    Science on the internet : a resource for K-12 teachers / Jazlin
V. Ebenezer, Eddy Lau.
        p.   cm
    Includes bibliographical references.
    ISBN 0-13-095918-9 (pbk.)
    1. Science—Study and teaching—Computer network resources.
    2. Internet (Computer network) in education.   I. Lau. Eddy.
    II. Title.
    LB1585.E189   1999
    507′ 1—dc21   98-33557
                                                                              CIP

Cover art: Diana Ong/Superstock
Editor: Bradley J. Potthoff
Production Editor: Mary M. Irvin
Design Coordinator: Diane C. Lorenzo
Cover Designer: Dan Eckel
Production Manager: Pamela D. Bennett
Production Coordination and Design: Elm Street Publishing Services, Inc.
Director of Marketing: Kevin Flanagan
Marketing Manager: Suzanne Stanton
Advertising/Marketing Coordinator: Krista Groshong

This book was set in Minion by The Clarinda Company and was printed and bound by
R. R. Donnelley & Sons Company. The cover was printed by Phoenix Color Corp.

 © 1999 by Prentice-Hall, Inc.
Simon & Schuster/A Viacom Company
Upper Saddle River, New Jersey 07458

Printed in the United States of America

10 9 8 7 6 5 4 3 2 1

ISBN: 0-13-095918-9

Prentice-Hall International (UK) Limited, *London*
Prentice-Hall of Australia Pty. Limited, *Sydney*
Prentice-Hall of Canada, Inc., *Toronto*
Prentice-Hall Hispanoamericana S. A., *Mexico*
Prentice-Hall of India Private Limited, *New Delhi*
Prentice-Hall of Japan, Inc., *Tokyo*
Simon & Schuster Asia Pte. Ltd., *Singapore*
Editora Prentice-Hall do Brasil, Ltda., *Rio de Janeiro*

For our mentor, colleague, and friend,
Dexter Harvey

For my loving son and Eddy's best friend,
Sudesh Ebenezer

PREFACE

As we approach a new century, more teachers are realizing that the Internet is the key to the Information Highway. The Internet is the center of a learning library where teachers as well as students can tap into on-line information resources anytime, anywhere.

In his 1998 State of the Union Address, U.S. President Bill Clinton challenged every school in the United States to install at least one computer in the school library that would have Internet access. The Internet is the ignition to systemic change for shaping students' opportunities for learning science. This book will assist you and your students in becoming better acquainted with resource materials available on the Internet for teaching and learning science.

Science on the Internet is in part a collection of science education Web sites useful for college students preparing to teach science, science teacher educators, teachers in the elementary, middle, and secondary classrooms, and students. Science content-based Web sites as well as Web sites pertaining to curricular topics, trends, and issues in science education are included. This collection also offers time-tested sites: government-sponsored, secure companies that we hope will be around for years to come. All of the sites have been reviewed carefully to ensure that content is useful and informational.

Chapter 1 describes briefly what the Internet is and how to use it. We have also provided you with a list of Internet tutorial sites that will teach you how to surf the Net. With the Yahoo! search engine, we also show you a way of narrowing Internet searches in science. This chapter, therefore, helps teachers to become Internet literate.

Chapter 2 presents a philosophy of science teaching for the 21st century. With the help of several screen captures from established Internet resources, we discuss how the Internet can be used in the context of science education. This chapter begins with two case studies of an elementary school science teacher and a high school science teacher using the Internet in their classrooms. It also suggests ways of integrating the Internet into science teaching. In particular, the sections on virtual field trips, conducting research, and joint classroom projects are valuable for science teachers and their students. Changes in the role of the teacher and the learner are examined, and criteria are listed for evaluating materials on the Internet.

Chapter 3 is the heart of the resource guide. It contains a wealth of resources that every science teacher will find useful. We have grouped each of the sites into categories that are similar to the topics outlined in the "science content standards" (National Research Council, 1996). The topical outline is as follows:

- Earth and Space Science
- Life Science

- Physical Science
- General Science
- Elementary Science
- Secondary Science
- K–12 Science
- Science, Technology, and Society Connections

Each of the suggested sites is annotated to provide content and insights about a particular homepage. Each of the entries in Chapter 3 is based on the following scale:

R	Rating (* = Average, ** = Very Good)
GL	Grade Level
TCK	Teacher Content Knowledge
RR	Research Reports
STS	Science Technology and Society
IL	Inquiry Lessons
RTD	Real Time Data

Chapter 4 is an electronic textbook. Teachers can find many sites that deal with current ideas concerning equity issues, for example.

The Appendixes include information on professional organizations and terms associated with the Internet. The Internet language will help you in your search.

A good assignment for prospective teachers is to review at least 10 sites from this book in an annotated WWW bibliography format, then to share those comments with all class members.

If the science education community reacts as positively to this handy guide as we think it will, we plan to update biennially.

ACKNOWLEDGMENTS

We kindly remember the technical assistance that Scott Wellman, Faculty of Education at the University of Manitoba, has continuously provided us. We acknowledge Dr. Joel Bass, Sam Houston State University, for providing us with materials on Real Time Data. We also thank all of our reviewers for their helpful suggestions to our initial draft: Joel Bass, Sam Houston State University; John R. Cannon, University of Nevada–Reno; and Joseph Peters, University of West Florida. We have attempted to incorporate their useful comments into this book.

Jazlin V. Ebenezer, Ed.D.
Eddy Lau, B.Sc.

CONTENTS

APPENDIXES

CHAPTER 1

Surfing the Netscape Browser

Source: Dr. Jazlin Ebenezer, University of Manitoba.

- The Internet
- Surfing the Internet
- Sites for Internet Guides and Tutorials
- Narrowing Searches for Net-Worthy Sites

THE INTERNET

The Internet is a huge network of interconnected computer networks linking the whole world (see Figure 1-1). For example, the computers in a college of education can be linked to form a network of computers. This is what is known as a LAN (local area network). This single network of computers is connected to other colleges in the same university, and the university computer network is then connected to a series of networks in other universities, school networks, commercial and business networks, government networks, industry networks, and every other network in the world, transcending geographical barriers. All of the computer networks have multilevel connections with telephone, radio, and satellite. Intercontinental telephone and fiberoptic connection lines running beneath the ocean floor link all the continents.

Figure 1-1   The Internet

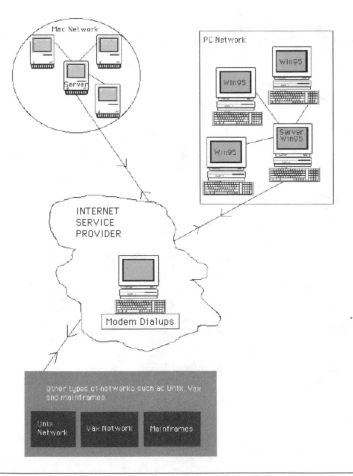

The Internet consists of information servers that include Web sites. An increasing number of Web sites are added each day to the Internet, thus making it more difficult to find relevant information. The emergence of search engines and search directories has harnessed the overflow of Web sites. With search engines and definitive subject and topic searches, information and resources on the Internet can be quickly located and extracted. The Netscape Browser provides a "graphic interface to the Internet and the World Wide Web allowing for exploration of information via hot buttons which link to further resources" (Morris, 1996). This shows you how to surf the Internet, connect to numerous sites, and communicate as well as collaborate!

What Is an Internet Address?

Each computer in the Internet is tagged or personalized with a set of numbers or letters, which is known as the IP (Internet Protocol) address. The Internet Protocol address enables you to search, locate, reach, and connect to a specific computer that provides the information for which you are looking. To find a Web site in the Internet, a set of syntax or procedures must be followed and this syntax connects to the computer that holds the particular information.

The Internet Web site address is called a URL, which stands for Uniform Resource Locator. An example of a URL for a Web site is:

http://home.cc.umanitoba.ca/~jazlin/guide/guide2.html

The standard format for a URL is:
protocol://host.domain[:port][/path][filename] in which

- the *protocol* is http (Hypertext Transport Protocol) for the http information server
- *host.domain* stands for home.cc.umanitoba.ca
- *path* represents /~jazlin/guide/
- *filename* stands for guide2.html

This standard format or syntax allows the browser client software to recognize and to make the appropriate connections to the location of the Web sites. This is somewhat similar to telephone or mail area codes.

Information Servers

On the Internet there are different types of information servers: *http, gopher, archie,* and *ftp.* These servers present information in different layouts and styles. *Http* features text, sound, graphics, and movie capabilities. In contrast, *gopher* and *archie* information servers are only text based.

Ftp (File Transfer Protocol) as the name indicates is a protocol for transferring files from one computer to another. But all servers use the same standard URL format. (See the section "What is an Internet Address?") If you need to change from one information server to another—for example, from the *http* information server to a *gopher* information server—change your protocol as follows: *from* **http://home.cc.umanitoba.ca/~jazlin/guide/guide2.html** *to* **gopher://gopher.cc.umanitoba.ca/**

SURFING THE INTERNET

How to Connect to a Web Site with a URL Address

1. *Type* the URL address in the "Go to" Box (sometimes referred to as the Location Box or Netsite Box) in the Netscape Browser.

> Go To : │http://home.cc.umanitoba.ca/~guide/guide2.│

2. *Press return.* You will be connected to the site. (See Figure 1-1.)

Steps to Search a Web Site of Your Choice

1. *Click* on the Net Search button on the Netscape Browser. You will see several search engines:
   - Excite
   - Infoseek
   - Lycos
   - Altavista
   - Magellan
   - Webcrawler

2. *Select* one of the search engines by clicking on it. You will see a rectangular box.

3. *Click* inside the box so that your cursor is in the box.

4. *Type* the subject or topic of your search in the rectangular box.

> Clouds K-6 Science   │ Search │

5. *Click* on the Search button as shown. You will now see a listing of "hits" of the topic or subject.

6. *Click* on the blue hypertext, also underlined in blue.

   Note: The links to the search engine are available in our support program.

Figure 1-2   Netscape

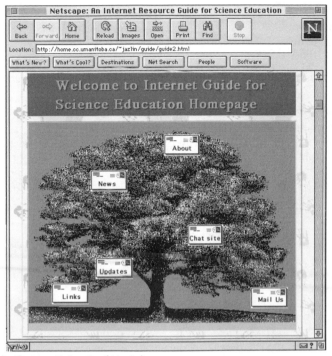

Source: Dr. Jazlin Ebenezer, University of Manitoba.

URL Address for Search Engine

Since the *Net Search* button (see Figure 1-2) is a link to all of the search engine sites, proper connections will not be made if the Net search server goes down. Therefore, we have provided you with the URL for each of the main search engines in the Internet (see Table 1-1).

Table 1-1   Addresses for the Main Search Engines in the Internet

Search Engine	URL
1. Altavista	http://altavista.digital.com/
2. Excite	http://www.excite.com/
3. Infoseek	http://www.infoseek.com/
4. Lycos	http://www.lycos.com/
5. Magellan	http://www.mckinley.com/
6. Webcrawler	http://www.webcrawler.com/

Choose a search engine from Table 1-1 and type the corresponding address in the Location Box in the Netscape Browser. Then repeat steps 2 through 6 described under "Steps to Search a Web Site of Your Choice."

Zones on the Internet

The URL consists of zones (see *com* and *ca* in the URL below) that represent the domain or the name of the host computer.

http://www.macromedia.*com*
http://www.umanitoba.*ca*

The term *com, edu,* or *ca* in the domain of the URL represents an organization or country (see Table 1-2):

Table 1-2   Zones and What They Represent

Zones	Representation
com	Commercial organization's homepage
edu	Educational organization's or institution's homepage
mil	Military-related site
net	Network organizations
org	Professional groups or institutions
int	International association or organization
gov	Government organization or agency
Ca (Canada)	Name of country

Downloading Information from the Internet onto Local Hard Drives

You can actually download resources from any of the information servers on the Internet to your hard drive or to a computer disk. This function is useful to minimize on-line costs in the Internet and to incorporate resources into your personal work.

Steps for Downloading Using a Macintosh Computer

1. *Click* with your mouse on the hypertext you want and hold. (Note: On the PC Windows 95 Operating Systems, the process is the same, but you have to click on the right button of your mouse and hold.)
   You will see a menu of options such as "save image as", "save link as", and "copy picture".
2. *Select* an option provided.
   You will see a box requesting you to specify where to put the downloaded file.

3. *Click* on the *Save* button to save either on the hard drive or on your personal disk.

SITES FOR INTERNET GUIDES AND TUTORIALS

There are guides and tutorials on the Internet that will assist you in surfing the Internet. Please go through the following URLs of Web sites if you want to learn more about surfing the Internet. To inform you as to what sorts of materials are available in the tutorial guides, we have included the table of contents for the first two electronic books listed.

Atlas to the World Wide Web
http://www.rhythm.com/~bpowell/Atlas/toc.htm

A virtual tour of the World Wide Web. Provides beginners with tutorials and guides. Listed below is the table of contents that is available on this site:

Introduction

Acknowledgments

Credits

Chapter 1: Welcome to Web-World

Before the Web
Origins of the Web: Some Basics
Who Travels the Web?
What Makes the Web a Web?
Managing Massive Web Growth
Just Browsing, Thanks

Chapter 2: Cruising Down the Web

Plugging In
Clients and Servers and Bears, Oh My!
Oh, What Tangled Webs We Weave
A Guide to Cyberspace

Chapter 3: Web Technology: Pay Attention to the Man Behind the Curtain

URIs, URLs, and URNs: A Rose by Any Other Name . . .
HTTP (HyperText Transfer Protocol)
Learning to Speak HTML
Linking to External Files
Entities, AKA Escape Sequences
To HTML or Not to HTML?
The Webmaster's Tool kit
WWW Developer Resources
To Weave, to Browse, or Merely to Roam?

The RoadMap to the Internet
URL: http://www.webreference.com/roadmap/

Covers the practical aspects of using the Internet. It is excellent for beginners.
Listed below is the table of contents available on this site:

WEEK 1

lesson	description
INTRO	ROADMAP96 INTRODUCTION
MAP01	WELCOME
MAP02	LISTSERV FILE SERVER COMMANDS

WEEK 2

lesson	description
MAP03	LEVELS OF INTERNET CONNECTIVITY
MAP04	E-MAIL
MAP05	LISTSERVS
MAP06	OTHER MAIL SERVERS
MAP07	NETIQUETTE

WEEK 3

lesson	description
MAP08	USENET
MAP09	SPAMMING AND URBAN LEGENDS
MAP10	INTERNET SECURITY
MAP11	TELNET (PART ONE)
MAP12	TELNET (PART TWO)

WEEK 4

lesson	description
MAP13	FTP (PART ONE)
MAP14	FTP (PART TWO)
MAP15	FTPMAIL
MAP16	FTP FILE COMPRESSION
MAP17	ARCHIE
MAP17B	FTP SITES

WEEK 5

lesson	description
MAP18	GOPHER (PART ONE)
MAP19	GOPHER (PART TWO)
MAP20	BOOKMARKS AND BOOKLISTS
MAP21	VERONICA
MAP22	GOPHERMAIL

WEEK 6

lesson	description
MAP23	WWW (PART ONE)
MAP24	WWW (PART TWO)
MAP25	ADDRESS SEARCHES AND FINGER
NEAT	MAP-EXTRA: NEAT STUFF TO CHECK OUT
ADVERT	ADVERTISING ON THE INTERNET
MAP26	IRC/MUDs/MOOs AND OTHER "TALKERS"
SMITH	GUEST LECTURER—RICHARD SMITH
MAP27	THE FUTURE . . .

Ask Dr. Internet
http://promo.net/drnet/

Extensive archive provides answers to common questions about the Web. Search for posting stories, or submit your own question.

Internet Web Text (Index)
http://www.december.com/web/text/index.html

Has a collection of most of the guides and tutorials that are available on the Internet.

Internet Guides, Tutorials, and Training Information
http://www.loc.gov/global/internet/training.html

Explore and download some of the documents that this library of Internet guides and tutorials offers in this Web site. Make sure you download the latest documents to get up-to-date information.

Internet Tour
http://info.globalvillag.com/gcweb/tour.html

An on-line tour of the Internet provides illustrations that make surfing easy for the beginner.

Internet Starter Kit
http://www.mcp.com/hayden/iskm/book.html

Connects to the latest Mac and Windows editions of the classic Internet guide that link to the best utilities and applications.

Internet 101
http://www2.famvid.com/i101/

Provides the basics on using the Net. Includes tips on searching, using e-mail, newsgroups, and chatrooms.

Jay Barker's Online Connection
http://www.barkers.org/online/

Compares major U.S. Internet service providers based on the connection's speed, price, software, features, and support.

Kid Safety
http://www.uoknor.edu/oupd/kidsafe/inet.htm

Provides step-by-step on-line tutorials and instructions on how children can use the Internet safely.

Learning Online
http://www.ualberta.ca/~maldridg/tutor/Tutorials.html

Provides a directory of Web-based tutorials for using the Internet, Web tools, Ethernet, and programming languages such as *Java*.

Life on the Internet
http://www.screen.com/start/welcome.html

This beginners' guide gives over 300 links as well as tips on using the browsers.

Mac Internet Connect Guide
http://www.i-55.com/mac2/

Provides step-by-step instructions for getting onto the Web. It has links to the necessary software and is primarily for novices but offers some tips for experts.

Netscape Tutorial
http://w3.aces.uiuc.edu/AIM/Discovery/Net/www/netscape/
index.html

Offers a step-by-step tutorial on how to use one of the finest WWW browsers available, the Netscape.

Netscape's Homepage
http://home.netscape.com/

This is Netscape's homesite. You can download Netscape's newest WWW browsers. You can also get Net tutorials and references in this site.

New Surfer's Guide
http://www.imagescape.com/helpweb/www/oneweb.html

Offers helpful articles on how to tour the Web and understand the terms used. Provides access to some useful starting points.

NSTA Online Resources
http://www.nsta.org/onlineresources/

This site provides extensive links to a variety of on-line resources such as html guides, Internet guides, and other sites that contain a huge collection of science and math lesson plans. You will be able to search on site for the type of resources that you are interested in obtaining.

New Users Resources
http://www.iah.com/newusers.html

Internet Access Houston provides access to useful software and applications and various tutorials for new Internet users.

New Users Guide
http://www.eskimo.com/~cher/eskimospace/Navigating.html

Provides information on helper applications and plug-ins and what they do for your computer. Covers chatrooms, telnet, e-mail, and the Usenet.

OSP Netscape Tutorial
http://www-osp.stanford.edu/Tutorial/tutorial.html

Includes a Netscape handbook for beginners and intermediate users of Netscape.

Polaris Internet Guide
http://users.southeast.net:80/~habedd/polaris/index.html

Contains an on-line tour or tutorial of the Internet. It also includes topics such as ISDN, FTP, WWW, and USENET.

Sites to See
http://www.wolinskyweb.com/jintro.htm

Resources and handouts from an introductory hands-on WWW workshop are available. Covers Web navigation and surfing.

The Internet Help Desk
http://w3.one.net/~alward/

This free guide helps both beginners and advanced Internet users. Covers e-mail, netiquette, and browsers.

The Online World Resources Handbook
http://www.simtel.net/simtel.net/presno/bok/

Offers help with starting points, Web page design, e-mail, and other facets of the Web.

The New Users directory
http://hcs.harvard.edu/~calvarez/newuser.html

Gives an introductory overview of the Web, features a rough guide to downloading software, and provides links to other starting points.

NARROWING SEARCHES FOR NET-WORTHY SITES

Let us use the search engine Yahoo! to search for possible science-related links. We will show you ways of narrowing searches using the **Yahoo! Site (http://www.yahoo.com/)**
Type: *K–12 science activities* in the *search* box.

Example 1: Exploring the Planets

The following site produced category matches (1–4 of 4):
http://search.yahoo.com/bin/search?p=k-12+science+activities
     This screen provides activities for science and mathematics education students. The bold-faced scripts are the hot links, and there are main science links and sub-links. Since we are interested only in science activities and lesson plans, we will click only on the science links.
     Science: Education: K–12: Activities is the first link on the screen
http://www.yahoo.com/Science/Education/K_12/Activities/
A click on this link showed a screen that had the following as the first link:

Interactive Activities (14)
http://www.yahoo.com/Science/Education/K_12/Activities/
     Interactive_Activities/

A click on this site led us to several links. We chose the following site:

Exploring the Planets
http://ceps.nasm.edu:2020/bestpics.html

This link gave us several links. One of them was as follows:

Observing Images
http://www.nasm.edu:2020/SIIMAGES/observin.html

A click on this link indicated links to many images. We selected the following link:

Image 16
http://www.nasm.edu:2020/SIIMAGES/image16.gif

This site was the end of the linkages.

Example 2: Science Learning Network

The following site produced category matches (1–4 of 4):
http://search.yahoo.com/bin/search?p=k-12+science+activities

1. **Science Education: K–12**
   http://www.yahoo.com/Science/Education/K_12/

2. **Science Learning Network**
   http://www.sln.org/

   A click on this site indicated several links. See 3a–3f. The computer screen also consisted of the following information:

   The Science Learning Network (SLN) is an on-line community of educators, students, schools, science museums, and other institutions demonstrating a new model for inquiry science education.

   SLN is also a 3-year, $6.5 million project funded by the National Science Foundation and Unisys Corporation. The project incorporates inquiry-based teaching approaches, telecomputing, collaboration among geographically dispersed teachers and classrooms, and Internet/World Wide Web content resources.

   SLN has established this Web site to support the project and the on-line community that is growing as a result. Below are the science museums and the "test-bed" schools that are the formal participants in the SLN project.

   Some of the SLN museum teams have also provided information.

   Exploratorium (San Francisco)
   Ross Elementary School

   The Franklin Institute (Philadelphia)
   Levering School

   Miami Museum of Science
   Avocado Elementary School

   Museum of Science (Boston)
   Hosmer School

   Oregon Museum of Science and Industry
   Buckman School

   Science Museum of Minnesota
   Museum Magnet School

3a. **Check out news and links**
    http://www.sln.org/now/index.html

3b. **Connect with schools and educators**
    http://www.sln.org/schools/index.html

3c. **Check out teacher and student projects**
http://www.sln.org/schools/projects/index.html

3d. **Visit our museums**
http://www.sln.org/museums/index.html

3e. **Explore our resources**
http://www.sln.org/resources/index.html

3f. **Find out about the network**
http://www.sln.org/info/index.html

A click on 3c leads to the Tropical Rain Forest. In the information on the Tropical Rain Forest, you will notice links to children's poetry:

Tropical Rain Forest
http://hosmer.watertown.k12.ma.us/WWW/snapolitano/rainforest/

Haiku Poetry
http://hosmer.watertown.k12.ma.us/WWW/snapolitano/rainforest/
　　haiku.html

Pyramid Poetry
http://hosmer.watertown.k12.ma.us/WWW/snapolitano/rainforest/
　　pyramid.html

Cinquain Poetry
http://hosmer.watertown.k12.ma.us/WWW/snapolitano/rainforest/
　　cinquain.html

Acrostic Poetry
http://hosmer.watertown.k12.ma.us/WWW/snapolitano/rainforest/
　　acrostic.html

Rain Forest Animals around the World
http://hosmer.watertown.k12.ma.us/WWW/snapolitano/rainforest/
　　ani_proj.html

Using the rainforest as a medium, the children learn the skills needed to research Rainforest Animals from Around the World. The children are also given the opportunity to apply their knowledge of rainforests by producing creative projects.
　　A click on 3b
(**Connect with schools and educators**
http://www.sln.org/schools/index.html) shows the Hosmer School.

The Hosmer School
http://hosmer.watertown.k12.ma.us/

From here you can go to *The Rain Forest,* which will take you through the previous links. The Hosmer School also offers other nice sites such as Dinosaur Picture Gallery, Whales, Butterflies, Ocean Animals Project, Multiage 4–5 Classroom, Multicultural Link, LiVirtual Field Trip to Lovells Is.

It was easy to narrow the sites for the information that we were looking for in the above examples because Yahoo! has a well-established hierarchy of science links.

CHAPTER SUMMARY

We have described what the Internet is and have shown you how to surf the Internet. In this chapter we also use the Yahoo! search engine to show how to narrow as well as identify Net-worthy sites in science. For detailed procedures on surfing, we have referred you to a number of sites where guides and tutorials are available. The choice is yours! Your technical literacy will improve if you master some of the specialized language that has been provided in the appendix. The Internet language is an important tool for communication.

References

Morris, J. L. (1996). *The technology revolution.* http://www.uvm.edu/~jmorris/
    comps2.html
Savetz, K. (1996). *The un-official Internet book list: Site indices & guides—Education.*
    http://www.northcoast.com/savetz/booklist/education.html

CHAPTER 2

Learning Science with the Internet

- Science Education Reform in a Technological World
- Internet Activities for Science: Case Studies
- Fourteen Ways of Using the Internet
- Student–Scientist Partnerships
- The Role of Teacher and Learner
- Criteria for Evaluating Materials

SCIENCE EDUCATION REFORM IN A TECHNOLOGICAL WORLD

Intellectual and communicative processes are integral to constructing and negotiating scientific knowledge. Collecting evidence, generating questions, and proposing and discussing explanations play major roles in scientific inquiry. A science class must reflect the inquiry processes that scientists conduct in their workplace, and a teacher must represent the scientific community (National Research Council, 1996). From a science-technology-society perspective, scientific knowledge and scientific ways of thinking are necessary for informed decision making. Collective decisions are essential to manage shared resources such as air, water, and forests. Workplaces expect workers to have the ability to be creative, to reason, to think, to make decisions, and to solve problems (National Research Council, 1996). In this whirl of change, how can we make science relevant for all students?

Developments in cognitive and social psychology as well as technology in the last decade have provided new perspectives on learning and have contributed to the systemic reform of school curricula and ways of teaching and assessing instruction. Learning is presently viewed as personal, social, and situational. Learning also depends upon attitudes, values, and interests of the learner. In line with these new developments, science education is focusing on lifelong learning and skill development that will enable our students to inquire, construct new ideas, wrestle with complexity, cope with uncertainty and ambiguity, adapt to constant change, solve conventional and unconventional problems, and develop a high degree of interpersonal and intrapersonal competence.

Christopher Dede, a professor of information technology, argues that new technological developments can help transform schools if these developments are used to support new models of teaching and learning, models that characterize sustained community-centered, constructivist classrooms for learner investigation, collaboration, and construction (O'Neil, 1995). The Internet and educational software can promote a collaborative culture in "doing science." For example, in student–scientist partnership programs, students are involved in large-scale projects such as **EARTHWATCH** and **GLOBE.** Students gather, analyze, and share data for questions that scientists ask. Science teachers explain science to their students as well as help students and scientists conduct their scientific inquiries (Cohen, 1997).

For developing appropriate scientific attitudes as well as attitudes toward science in children, teachers' understanding of the nature of scientific inquiry is crucial because children's attitudes toward science are formed at a young age and are determined by teaching style and methods (Hofstein & Welch, 1984; Jegede, 1989; Kelly, 1988). The Internet provides teachers the opportunity to use several teaching methods in their classrooms and also helps to shape children's conceptions about science and what scientists do.

INTERNET ACTIVITIES FOR SCIENCE: CASE STUDIES

The Internet: What is it? Do we need it? Is it useful? Should I learn how to use it? Should I implement Internet-based information in my class? These are the questions science teachers frequently ask.

In the past, school activities and teachers' role modeling shaped children's conceptions about science, and students learned science through authorized/prescribed textbooks. But the Internet has now become a major force in shaping young minds, and teachers who use Internet technology in their science classrooms know the potential benefits and values that technology brings to the overall learning of their science students.

How can you teach in a knowledge-intensive society? This is a challenge for most teachers—a reason we turn to computers and the Information Superhighway, the Internet. Young people are expected to be fluent in information literacy skills in the workplace, and we think science education is an appropriate context where some of the skills can be developed. Science education's on-line world enables children to explore a new set of experiences. The Internet is a new resource that can be explored and meaningfully used to help satisfy children's curiosity. Through experts' knowledge, it provides answers to questions that children ask. What are the potential uses of the Internet in a science classroom? In the following section we narrate two case studies: the case study of Joel Bass, a science teacher educator (private correspondence), and the case study of Marlene Kroeker, a school teacher (Kroeker, 1997).

The Internet for Real Time Data

I am currently doing a lab which requires the use of real time tide data from National Oceanographic & Atmospheric Administration (NOAA). Students have to go to San Francisco and other sites to collect data throughout the day. This data is submitted to an on-line database on my machine from which they develop and retrieve data and develop charts and graphs. This type of activity uses the power of the Internet. [Joel Bass, a science teacher educator at Sam Houston University]

The Internet has been an important means for scientists at multiple sites to collaborate in research projects. Just as the Internet has been productive in scientific research, the Internet can be an excellent tool in the science classroom in promoting a constructivist approach to interactive exploration and learning. By bringing interesting and significant information into the classroom, technology can provide effective enrichments that might not be possible otherwise.

The New Jersey Networking Infrastructure in Education (NJNIE) project has taken a lead in developing on-line activities for students (Friedman, Baron, and Addison, 1996). In NJNIE Internet activities, the focus is on analysis of quantitative data that is emerging from current sources. Through working with data from the Internet, students not only deepen their knowledge of science but also increase their mathematical skills as they encounter the precise order, regularity, and predictability that is inherent in the natural world.

NJNIE has done valuable preliminary work in designing activities that suggest how Internet data sources might be used in science classes. Consider the NJNIE activity on Ships at Sea as an example. If you have Internet access now, you might wish to examine the **Ships at Sea** site at the URL address: http://njnie.dl.stevens-tech.edu/curriculum/currichome.html

Hundreds of ships in the world's oceans regularly report their precise locations along with basic information about weather and water conditions. Ocean Weather, Inc., maintains a database on this information, updating it several times each day. Ships are designated by IDs; locations of each ship are given by latitude and longitude and can also be seen on an Ocean Graphic map. The shear volume of data can be overwhelming, but it becomes manageable within the context of engaging elementary or middle-school students in problems related to vicarious travel. Students pretend they are stowaways on a ship with a given ID. The stowaways wonder where they are going and when they will arrive. Somehow they obtain access to the Internet. Referring to sequential reports of their ship's location given on the Internet, students map their trip and try to predict the location of the port to which the ship is bound. Internet sources linked to the Ships at Sea site can also be used to determine how far the ship has traveled between two specific locations. Using the distance information and time data drawn from the ship's reports, students can calculate the ship's rate of speed. With this information and calculations of the distance from their current location to the destination port, students can estimate their time of arrival. The whole scenario is presented as a problem, with students having to determine which concepts are relevant and how the concepts are to be used.

Activities somewhat similar to NJNIE's Ships at Sea can be carried out with data on the locations of whales given on the **Whale Net** Web site. The URL address of this site is

http://whale.Wheelock.edu/

Source: J. Michael Williamson, Whalenet, Wheelock College.

Similar to the Ships at Sea database, Whale Net provides information on the date and location (latitude and longitude) for each sighting of a white whale named Rat. A black-and-white map of the ocean is provided for mapping data on Rat's movements. Students can enter the latitude and longitude data for two points on the map into a "Distance Generator," which is provided at a site linked to Whale Net, and determine how far apart the points are. In an in-service project for middle-school math and science teachers, participants were encouraged to formulate and address different questions about Rat's movement. Some questions addressed by the teachers were: What was the maximum distance Rat traveled in one day? What was his maximum speed? Are weather and water conditions related to the fact that Rat seems to linger near particular locations? The teachers worked to answer the questions through analysis of the data available on the Internet.

A great deal of data on sunspots is also available on the Internet. Images of the sun can be studied from the National Oceanographic & Atmospheric Administrations's site.

Source: NOAA Office of Public Affairs, U. S. Dept. of Commerce.

http://www.noaa.gov

This site shows sunspots as well as the latitudes and longitudes of their positions on the surface of the sun.

The Internet facilitates new types of interesting, intellectually significant educational tasks that are not likely to reach learners via other methods. Through databased Internet activities, students at all levels can engage in the constructive types of explorations that are common among scientists.

The Internet Access for Science Fairs

Do the words science fair *fill you with dread and anxiety? Do you wish for a plan that could eliminate science fair stress? For many elementary school educators, science fair time is just one big headache. My first rounds at science fairs were not a good experience . . . for me (my students seemed to enjoy themselves). Until one year I spent some time to develop an 8-week science fair "game plan." [Kroeker, 1997]*

How does Marlene Kroeker begin science fair projects in her class? How does she use Internet activities for science fairs? Marlene takes an eight-week block to help her students with science fair projects during science and language arts classes.

Getting Started

Science Fairs

Source: Science World—British Columbia, Canada.

Science world
http://www.scienceworld.bc.ca/SCIENCEFAIRS/SFLinks.html

This site is an encouraging homepage for answering the question, "How can science fairs provide great learning opportunities?"

The TeacherLounge
http://www.scienceworld.bc.ca/SCIENCEFAIRS/SFTeacherLounge.html

This site suggests advice for organizing the actual science fair and some project ideas.

Science Project
http://www.scienceworld.bc.ca/SCIENCEFAIRS/SFGetStart.html

This site gets you started with science fairs.

As a class Marlene and her students visit How to Do a Science Fair Project.

Marlene states "This site is very eye-catching and gives simple, well-detailed information for every step of the project." The related appropriate sites are as follows:

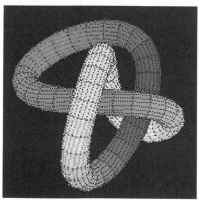

Source: Dr. Larry Dennis, Florida State University.

Practical Hints for Science Fair Projects
http://www.scri.fsu.edu/~dennisl/special/sf_hints.html

Source: Science World—British Columbia, Canada.

The Nature of the Science Fair Project
http://www.scienceworld.bc.ca/SCIENCEFAIRS/SFNature.html

A Student Check-List
http://www.scienceworld.bc.ca/SCIENCEFAIRS/SFCheckList.html

This site provides a working outline.

The Mad Scientist's Why Write
http://oakview.fcps.edu:80/~glazewsk/96-97/scientist/why-write.html

This site discusses why it is important to maintain journal accounts of daily experimental work.

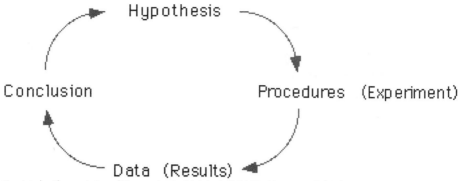

Reprinted with permission of Gregory Lock, Prinicipal, Oak View Elementary School.

Scientific Method
http://oakview.fcps.edu:80/~glazewsk/96-97/scientist/method.html

This site outlines the scientific method that students can follow.

Reprinted with permission of Gregory Lock, Prinicipal, Oak View Elementary School.

Small Things Glossary
http://oakview.fcps.edu:80/~glazewsk/96-97/
scientist/glossary.html#hypothes

This is useful for science terms.

Reprinted with permission of Gregory Lock, Prinicipal, Oak View Elementary School.

The Mad Scientist Special Topics
http://oakview.fcps.edu:80/~glazewsk/96-97/scientist/experiments.html

This site shows simple experiments.

Source: © Nybor Corporation.

Showboard
http://www.showboard.com/science/science.htm

This site lists project ideas by grade level. A small cost is attached to it.

After students have identified project ideas, they are ready to make a problem statement. The problem statement is written in the form of a question in their journal. Sample questions for experiments are available in the following site:

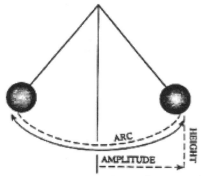

Reprinted with permission of Gregory Lock, Prinicipal, Oak View Elementary School.

The Mad Scientist's Pendulums
http://oakview.fcps.edu:80/~glazewsk/96-97/
    scientist/pendulum/amp/index.html

Visit Completed Science Fairs on the Internet

It is important that students read other students' work as they continue to do their own projects.

Grade 8 Science Fair
http://www2.excite.sfu.ca/pgm/scifair/pgmsci.html

This site has three completed projects using the scientific method.

Statement of Hypothesis

Students should be reading, Internet surfing, interviewing experts, etc., about their topics to formulate a statement of hypothesis and reasons for their hypothesis.

Hypothesis
http://oakview.fcps.k12.va.us:80/~ glazewsk/96-97/scientist/

Experimental Organization

Students should organize the material for their experiments, write up the method, and identify the independent and controlled variables. See the following two sites:

Showboard
http://www.showboard.com/science/sfd01.htm

This site has a science fair demonstration kit that can give students ideas for their experiments and finished products.

Science Fairs and Students
http://www.scienceworld.bc.ca/SCIENCEFAIRS/SFStudent.html

Experimentation and Observation

Students do the experiments and conduct fair texts for comparing results. They make careful observations that they record in a chart or graph. Then they write conclusions to the problem. Was the hypothesis correct?

Finding Judges and Awards

Ribbons, Certificates, and Buttons
http://www.showboard.com/science/science.htm

This site provides suggestions for finding judges and selecting awards.

Backboard

Science Fair—Making a Backboard
http://www.scienceworld.bc.ca/SCIENCEFAIRS/SFDisplay.html

This site provides information for creating a backboard.

Science Fair Backboard Directions
http://trms.k12.fulton.ga.net/~docallag/sci-fair/SciFBackboard.html

This site provides a diagram and layout of a backboard.

Marlene's e-mail address is mkroeker@mbnet.mb.ca and she hopes that this Web tour has helped with science fair planning. She wants you to write to her if you have any suggestions or ideas to add to science fair preparation.

FOURTEEN WAYS OF USING THE INTERNET

Testing Personal Ideas

Constructivist science teaching involves the teacher preparing a lesson or activity to clarify or elaborate students' ideas. At the second level students themselves will be looking for ideas to test their own conceptions. The Internet is a great source for excellent science activities to test personal ideas.

The Internet contains thousands of science activities in all science content areas: earth and space science, life science, and physical science.

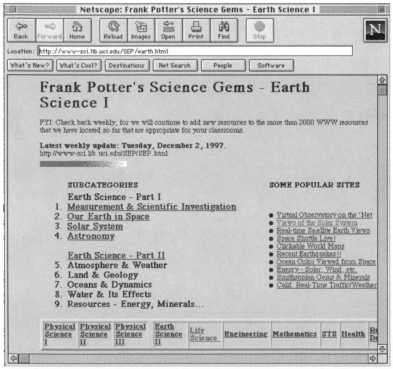

Reprinted with permission of Frank Potter, University of California—Irvine, SEP Assoc. Director.

Frank Potter's Science Gems—Earth Science
http://www-sci.lib.uci.edu/SEP/earth.html

This site categorizes more than 2,000 earth science links.

© *New Jersey Online.*The Yuckiest Site on the Internet, front page graphics of Website, at
http://www.nj.com/yucky/

The Yuckiest Site in the Internet
http://www.nj.com/yucky/

This site is a New Jersey Online and the Liberty Science Center collaborative work.
This site features multimedia classroom activities and information about worms
and cockroaches for grades K–6. There are more than 100 physical science lessons
for K–12 in **Physical Science Lessons** (http://www.eecs.umich.edu/mathscience/
funexperiments/agesubject/physicalsciences.html).

Reprinted with permission of Mid-Continent Regional Educational Lab.

Whelmers Home Page
http://www.mcrel.org/whelmers/

This site features examples of lesson plans based on *National Science Education Standards*. Any of these lessons and activities, appropriately chosen, can be used either to clarify or elaborate students' conceptions.

Conducting Internet Labs

For the investigation of the cell and photosynthesis, a group of students used URL: http://lenti.med.umn.edu/~mwd/cell_WWW/chapter1/cell_chapter1.html. Students examined the information on **Prokaryotes** and **Eukaryotes** and answered the following questions:

1. Compare the eukaryotes with the prokaryotes using the information on the Internet. Add it to your notes.

2. Find drawings of the Bacterium and Cyanophyte. Draw and label these cells.

3. Discuss the cell diagram. Find an organelle that we did not discuss in class. Name this organelle. Click on the organelle and write a brief description of it.

4. How are these organelles unlike lysosomes?

5. Click on the rest of the structures on this cell and record any information that will help add to your class notes.

6. Find information about the plasma membrane and the function of the cholesterol in the lipid bilayer (Timmons et al., 1997)

Taking a Virtual Trip

Children can visit a zoo or science center from the classroom even if field trips are not possible. This is what makes the Internet so beneficial: The Internet provides a virtual experience. Adventures, experiments, field trips, and museums are within children's reach through the Internet.

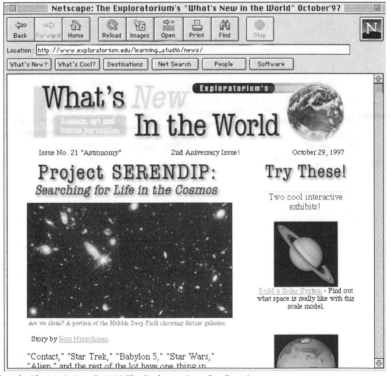

Reproduced with permission. © 1998 The Exploratorium, San Francisco.

The Exploratorium
http://www.exploratorium.edu/learning_studio/news/

This site is a San Francisco–based interactive science museum that hosts on-line experiments. Have the experience of performing hands-on science at this site: (http://www.exploratorium.edu/light _walk/pinhole_todo.html).

Source: NASA Goddard Space Flight Center.

SeaWiFS Project
http://seawifs.gsfc.nasa.gov/SEAWIFS.html

This site belongs to NASA's Goddard Space Flight Center. It provides a teacher's guide featuring on-line activities with answers so that high school students can study ocean color from space. The topics include life in the ocean, the ocean isn't just blue, phytoplankton, the earth, and carbon.

Conducting Research

Starting from the age of 12, most young people can use the research resources of the Internet. They can have access to scientific information from the Library of Congress's collection, ERIC, journals, magazines, and newspapers. For example,

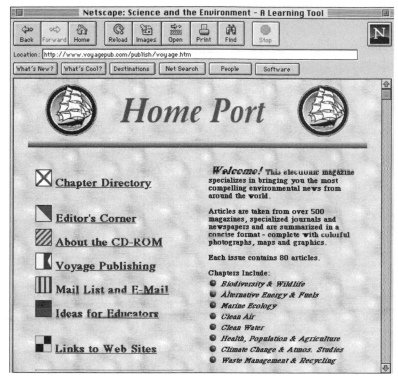

Reprinted with permission of Voyage Publishing, Inc.

Science and the Environment
http://www.voyagepub.com/publish/voyage.htm

This site is an electronic magazine that brings environmental news from all over
the world. Articles are taken from over 500 magazines, specialized journals, and
newspapers. These articles are complete with colorful photographs, maps, and
graphics. Scientific information may also be obtained from informal learning institutions such as museums and space agencies.

Home of NASA's Quest Project

HOT TOPICS

Source: NASA Ames Research Center.

NASA sites
http://quest.arc.nasa.gov/

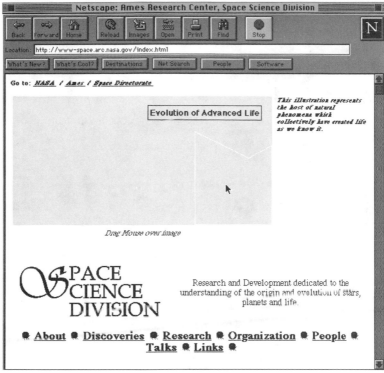

Source: NASA Ames Research Center.

http://www-space.arc.nasa.gov/index.html/

Source: NASA.

http://www.nasa.gov/

contain "information on all of the space agency's programs, an on-line library for research, and exhibits on recent space phenomena, such as the comets, Hubble Telescope, MIR, and the Galileo spacecraft. If you are interested in the Space Shuttle, there are special pages for all of its missions, including information on weather and orbits, a tour, and a special countdown page" (Lazarus & Lipper, 1996).

Although NASA is taking the lead, NOAA, the Department of Energy, National Institutes of Health (NIH), and many more agencies have good research data available for students to work with on the Internet. The butterfly migrations and acid rain projects were seen by educators and the public as two of the most effective uses of the Internet.

Participating in Joint Classroom Projects

Science teachers and students can collaborate their thoughts, ideas, or questions with other science teachers and students across the world on the Internet. This will give teachers and students a wider understanding of a particular topic and the many aspects of learning to solve a problem.

Teachers involved in a collaborative project can engage students in a joint or common project. **Creative Futures** (http://www.ozemail.com.au/~michaels/

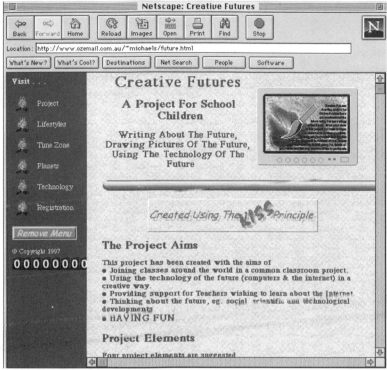

Source: Creative Futures Project—Michael Schofield, Project Coordinator.

future.html) involves students joining classes around the world in a common classroom project via computers and the Internet. The program encourages children to write and draw about the future in society, science, and technology using the technology of the future. Classrooms are encouraged to share their work using the Internet.

Communicating Ideas

Children can chat with experts in scientific fields as well as peers worldwide through listservs or e-mail discussion groups. There are numerous listservs where students and teachers can ask questions and share and communicate common knowledge and interests. Examples of listservs are **fish ecology** (listserv@searn.sunet.se), **educational technology** (listserv@msu.edu), **elementary education** (listserv@ksuvm.bitnet), and **multimedia** (listserv@unlvm.unl.edu).

In 1997, a Russian class wanted to exchange observations about local plant life with 10 to 15 American boys and girls. The Russian class's search was as follows:

From: root@licey-kupol.altai.ru

To: iecc@stolaf.edu

Subject: Seeking US secondary class for partnership watching for plants' lives

IECC is an international and intercultural classroom e-mail partnership facility in which primary and secondary teachers exchange ideas with other teachers.

E-mail journal writing has also become a way in which students share their thoughts, ideas, and questions with their teachers and peers. Both teachers and students must be electronically organized because their e-mail mailboxes can get flooded.

With the emergence of Internet communication software such as Cu-SeeMe, Internet Phone, and Cooltalk, as well as with the companion hardware QuickCam (a small, ball-shaped camera for the computer), teachers and students can collaborate through Video-Image live on the Internet. No matter where you are in the world, you can talk to the person and see that person on your computer, making distance education a reality at minimal cost. With Internet Phone and Cooltalk, teachers and students around the world can talk long distance free of charge on the Internet. Collaboration and sharing of ideas and information can be done swiftly, effectively, and cost free.

Asking Experts

Children are naturally curious. They come up with interesting questions, and some of their questions are challenging. This is one of the opportunities to direct the student to an expert scientist. The Mad Scientist Network, on the next page, is an excellent example of a site that allows children to get answers to their science-related questions.

Reprinted with permission of Washington University School of Medicine.

MAD Scientist Network
http://medicine.wustl.edu:80/~ysp/MSN/MAD.SCI.html

This site is a collective cranium of scientists from around the world fielding questions in different areas of science. The scientists will answer students' questions, and this will help children with their homework and research projects. As a teacher you may also become a member of this Network to answer students' questions.

Collaborating with Scientists

As a teacher you can find out about the events in your science areas.

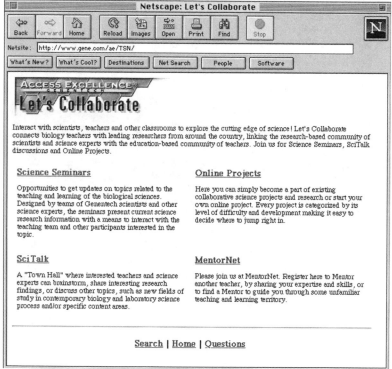

Reprinted with permission of Genentech, Inc.

Let's Collaborate
http://www.gene.com/ae/TSN/

This site allows you and your students to interact with scientists, teachers, and other classrooms to explore the cutting edge of science. It connects biology teachers with leading researchers from around the USA, linking the research-based community of scientists and science experts with the education-based community of teachers. Join Let's Collaborate for science seminars, scitalk discussions, and on-line projects.

Source: Ecologic Corporation.

The Earth Systems Science Community Curriculum Testbed
http://www.circles.org/

This project links students and teachers in high schools and universities in an effort to build an earth system science community. This site illustrates how electronic technology can support collaboration among scientists and students.

Students and scientists communicate via e-mail and computer conferencing. This telementoring is useful for project-based teaching and learning. CoVis Project (1993) at Northwestern University provides a volunteer telementoring service to secondary students with long-term science projects. Following is an excerpt from an e-mail exchange between a secondary student and a graduate student about earthquake research.

> *Thursday, 2 May 1996*
> *Dear Mary,*
> *We are juniors at New Trier High School. We are participating in a group project involving earthquakes. Your help would be greatly appreciated. Our project is due on May 17.*
> *Yours Truly, Marilyn and Robert*

Dear Marilyn and Robert,
Hello and welcome! Glad to hear from you. I'm really excited about working with
you on this project. Whew! Tight time line, but I'm sure we can make it. What
aspect of earthquakes are you interested in? We first need to define the
question/info that best graphs your interest, and then we can formulate a research
attack plan for the project. Draft a few ideas on paper, then e-mail me back with
the info. Once we have a good topic, we can hit the ground running. If you're
short on ideas, grab the local paper or the [Chicago] *Tribune, or news magazines*
like Time, Newsweek, *or even* Discover. *With the recent earthquake in the Pacific*
Northwest, I'm sure the media has cooked up a few articles with cool graphics.
(O'Neill, Wagner, Gomez, 1996, p. 39)

Rich conversation and learning take place when projects are challenging and
interesting and sufficient time is given to students to complete the project. Teachers recruit telementors by posting a message on the Usenet newsgroups and listservs dedicated to scientific research. Subsequently, teachers describe the project
and their expectation of students to the volunteering telementors through e-mail.
The success of telementoring depends on the commitment of both the telementee
and the telementor, time given to telementors for their feedback to students, and
the teacher's ongoing communication with telementors and students.

Sharing Classroom-Based Work

"The World Wide Web (WWW) is the world's largest bulletin board" (Morris,
1996). You may have arrived at an original lesson idea. Consider sharing your lesson plans or activity on the Internet. Other teachers will be able to find out what
you are doing in your science class. Likewise, you may also examine other teachers'
curricula by visiting appropriate Internet sites. You will find them to be worthwhile
in preparing for teaching and assessing children's understanding. For example, the
Keep America Beautiful site

Reprinted with permission of Keep America Beautiful, Inc.

Keep America Beautiful Homepage
http://www.kab.org/

provides educational information on solid waste management (recycling, composting, waste-to-energy, sanitary, landfilling) and litter prevention. It also offers lesson plans and other on-line publications. For alternative assessment, visit the following site.

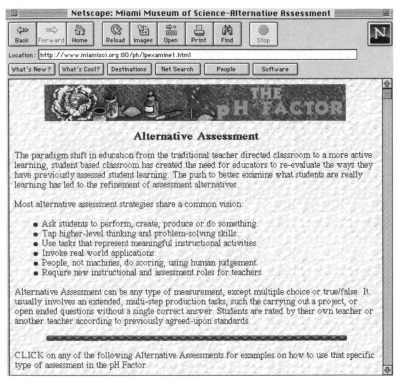

Reprinted with permission of Miami Museum of Science.

Miami Museum of Science—Alternative Assessment
http://www.miamisci.org:80/ph/lpexamine1.html

Types of alternative assessment covered in this site are performance-based, authentic or project, portfolio, and journal. Each of these types of assessment is graphically illustrated by using the pH Factor. Within the journal section, Howard Gardner's theory of multiple intelligence is illustrated.

You may also consider asking students to share their multimedia projects involving science–technology–society-related issues on the Internet. We have witnessed elementary as well as secondary students creating their own multimedia projects using texts, graphics, sound, video, and animation using *PowerPoint, HyperCard, HyperStudio,* and *Persuasion.* These projects also contain links to Internet-based information using a text editor. Rodelyn Stoeber, a high school science teacher, states:

> *In my classes, the students have used the Internet to research information for research topics in physics and in my grade 10 science courses. For example, for a research project on cancer, the students were given a scenario in which either themselves or a significant other was facing the threat of a type of cancer. In a letter or journal format, the students had to describe what they were going through.*

In order to do this, the students had to research the type of cancer using a variety of resources, one of which was the Internet. Students had to be reminded that they needed to cross reference any material that they found on the Internet since not all information is reliable or accurate.

My physics students created Web pages based on historical figures who contributed significantly to discoveries in physics. Students chose to document the lives of people like Stephen Hawking, Isaac Newton, or Aristotle. Students also created Web pages for Vincent Massey Collegiate's "Adopt A River: Seine River Project." Here, students amassed the information that they got from field trips, guest speakers, and their own research to put together Web pages that could also be used for presentation purposes.

(e mail from Rodelyn Stoeber, February 24, 1997)

Also on the Internet you will find teachers sharing their classroom projects with the rest of the world. Your students can access these for their own learning.

Creating an Electronic Portfolio

An electronic portfolio is an interactive multimedia approach to organizing your learning experiences in the on-line environment. You can use multimedia software such as *HyperStudio, Hypercard,* and *Kid Pix* to create and manage an electronic portfolio. Your portfolio can include text, graphics, sound, animation, and video to represent as well as share what you have learned.

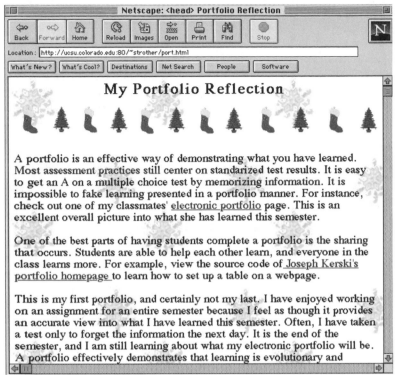

Reprinted with permission of Cheri Strothers, University of Colorado.

My Portfolio Reflection
(http://ucsu.colorado.edu:80/~strother/port.html)

This site is an example of an electronic portfolio. **Electronic Portfolio** (http:// mailer.fsu.edu:80/~jflake/assign.html) offers suggestions for developing an electronic portfolio. **Why Electronic Portfolio Assessment** (http:// www.cs.binghamton.edu:80/~loland/why.html) discusses the benefits of electronic portfolio assessment: "Easier to keep track of student information, reduces storage needs, and a simple and fast interface to find information."

See more sites on assessment in chapter 4.

Using Time Efficiently

Science teachers and students can learn anytime from any location via the Internet. **Cool School Tools!** (http://199.76.61.8:80/cooltools/), a service of Birmingham Public Library and Cherokee Regional Library, is an index to the World Wide Web and other Internet resources for children and teenagers in grades K–12. Teachers can ask students to do an activity (e.g., Seltzer Tablet Rocket) and discuss what they have learned.

Learning in a Relaxed Environment

The Internet gives science students the choice of learning in a relaxed environment. Students are not rushed and challenged by peer pressure to learn as quickly as their peers. Teachers also have the luxury of using lesson plans and activities available on the Internet in their classrooms rather than wondering where to get lessons and activities on a particular topic. They also have access to novel ideas of teaching and learning. For example, **EUREKA** is the Premier Site for Science Educational Discoveries (http://cybershopping.com/eureka/eureka.html). Eureka has lesson plans on:

Chromatography of Leaf Pigments

Do You Believe Your Eyes? A Hands-On Inquiry Investigation

Using Hydrophobic Sand

An Investigation Using Owl Pellets

Colorful Capsules—A Hands-On Inquiry Investigation

Does Color Affect the Burning Time of Birthday Candles?

These lesson plans include scientific inquiry as well as alternative ways of assessing student learning.

Motivating Students

Attractive graphics, animation, sound, and movie clips in Web pages motivate students to use the Internet. This contrasts with textbook learning. For example, **Insanely Great Science Websites** sponsored by The Science Club, Inc. (http://www.eskimo.com/~billb/amateur/coolsci.html), will motivate even unmotivated science students.

Simulating Dangerous and Costly Experiments

The Internet enables simulations of dangerous and costly classroom science experiments, allowing science teachers to play "What if I do this experiment?" with students. Students will also see immediate results of the experiment on the Internet. (Example: http://www.seattleu.edu./~khouston/science.html.)

STUDENT–SCIENTIST PARTNERSHIPS

Student–scientist partnerships, as the name implies, bring science and education together, and students learn both the content and the process of science. While scientists and experts engage students in collecting data to answer their questions, students have the opportunity to work closely with scientists in their actual studies. Students also have the added advantage of using the instruments scientists use. Hence, it is a mutual benefit, and students in both school settings and nonformal settings can collaborate with scientists. For example, David Tucker, a physics and biochemistry teacher at Mount Baker High School in Washington state, engages his students in environmental research projects.* These students focus on "lead, zinc, phosphates, and nitrates in the soils, lakes, streams, and ground water to determine the health of salmon habitats. Students design valid investigations like the practicing scientists do and process their results similarly" (Cohen, 1997, p. 7). For additional details about student–scientist partnership projects, we invite you to consult the excellent book entitled *Internet Links for Science Education,* edited by Karen C. Cohen.

The GLOBE Program
http://www.globe.gov/

Global Learning and Observations to Benefit the Environment (GLOBE) is a worldwide network of K–12 students, teachers, and scientists working together to study and understand the global environment. GLOBE students make environmental observations near their schools. Students learn how to observe the environment by making scientific measurements of air temperature, precipitation, water temperature, and pH. Students then send their findings to the GLOBE Student Data Archive via the Internet. Scientists use GLOBE data in their research and provide feedback to the students to enrich their science education. For example, GLOBE students are tracking El Niño. GLOBE students can help quantify the effects of El Niño around the world.

Source: Peter Scheifele, NOAA National Undersea Research Center, University of Connecticut.

The Aquanaut Program
http://www.ucc.uconn.edu/~wwwnurc/apintr.html

Note: David Tucker was the cooperating teacher of Jazlin Ebenezer, the senior author of this Internet guide, in 1976–1977 at Mount Baker High School in Washington state.

The Aquanaut Program is an innovative educational initiative of NOAA's National Undersea Research Center at the University of Connecticut at Avery Point. High school students and teachers experience the marine environment working under the guidance of a mentor scientist. This program gives teachers opportunities to improve their science research skills by participating in a research project and stresses a hands-on approach to learning. Students and teachers apply scientific methodologies in problem solving. The at-sea experience requires a multidisciplinary approach.

Boreal Forest Watch!
http://www.bfw.sr.unh.edu/

BFW is an environmental monitoring educational outreach program that is Sasketchewan based for Canadian high school teachers and their students. The activities include site selection and sampling plot layout, sample tree selection and identification, tree diameter, tree height and height of live crown, and tree form and diagnosis. The optional activities include: anatomical investigations, chlorophyll content determination, temperature data collection, and precipitation data collection.

Particles and Prairies
http://www-ed.fnal.gov/Samplers/prairie/pp.html

Particles and Prairies is a collaborative project between teachers and scientists that provides middle-school students the experience of being scientists. Students gather data and make observations of the prairie. This data collection helps the ongoing prairie restoration project at Fermilab.

Particles and Prairies provides students a close, hands-on look at the abiotic and biotic aspects of the prairie, the savannah, and the aquatic environments of Fermilab. Teachers must attend a workshop in order to schedule field trips for their students to do both lab and field studies at Fermilab.

Give Water a Hand
http://www.uwex.edu/erc/index.html

Give Water a Hand is a national watershed education program. In this project young people take action to improve local water quality. They team up with educators, natural resource experts, and committed community members to study water issues and take action! Materials are free and can be downloaded when you register.

The Rivers Project
http://www.siue.edu/OSME/river/

Scientific literacy is the goal of The Rivers Project. American and Canadian teachers have been trained in this project. Students collect and analyze water samples from various test state agencies and give them to the Environmental Management Technical Center. River study includes historical, social, and/or economic implications of the river conditions, thus involving students from classes across the curricular areas of science, mathematics, social studies, and language arts.

High School Human Genome Program
http://chroma.mbt.washington.edu/outreach/hgp.html

Scientists and local high school teachers have developed a program that allows students to participate in sequencing small portions of the human genome: Students sequence unsequenced DNA. The results are placed in the appropriate national scientific databases. Students also discuss the ethical and social issues that arise from advances in the genome project. During a 1-week summer institute held in the MBT teaching laboratory, teachers receive the training necessary to carry out the project in their classrooms. Equipment and technical support are provided during the school year. This program is funded by the Department of Energy.

Project Feeder Watch
http://birdsource.cornell.edu/pfw.htm

Project Feeder Watch is a winter survey of the birds that visit backyard feeders in North America. The information collected each year helps ornithologists track changes in the abundance and distribution of bird species that use feeders in the winter. Goals of Project Feeder Watch are:

Gather long-term data on winter bird populations throughout North America.

Detect significant population declines or expansions.

Track the dynamic movements of nomadic and irruptive species during the winter months.

Identify habitat features (including types of feeders and artificial foods) that attract or enhance bird populations.

Involve bird watchers in serious ornithological study.

Provide direct feedback to project participants and the general public regarding bird population trends.

EnviroNet
http://earth.simmons.edu/

EnviroNet is a network of students, teachers, scientists, environmental educators, and others who utilize telecommunication technology to enhance environmental science education in the K–12 community throughout New England and the nation. The **BirdWatch** site at http://earth.simmons.edu/birdwatch/birdwatch_activities.html is part of EnviroNet. BirdWatch includes classroom activities, student publications, links to resources, etc. BirdWatch activities include construction of bird feeders using plastic milk jugs and milk cartons.

THE ROLE OF TEACHER AND LEARNER

Technology has greatly influenced the way teachers teach and how learners learn science because the Internet "holds the whole world in its hands." It puts teachers and students in a collaborative research mode. Students often teach themselves because they have in-depth knowledge about a topic as a result of their research via the Internet. This might be threatening to a traditional teacher because the power is shifted to the student. However, the responsibility of constructing knowledge must be rightfully returned to the learner!

With the use of the Internet's resources, teachers can put into practice Howard Gardner's theory of Multiple Intelligences very effectively, thus meeting the needs and interests of students. Students do not have to be locked into space, time, and resources. For example, Updegrove (1995) reports in the Apple Classrooms of Tomorrow (ACOT) research project in which high school students had many opportunities to use computers and networks to enhance their learning:

> . . . students had significant growth in their independence and their ability to be collaborative problem solvers and communicators. . . . Teachers have shifted their educational approach from one of knowledge transfer (instructionism) to one of knowledge building (constructivism). Classroom instruction shifted from traditional lecture model to one that depended heavily on student collaboration and peer teaching (Apple Education Research Series, summary as cited in Updegrove, 1995).

Computers put the students in the ACOT project in contact with resources worldwide. The teacher's responsibility for stimulating students' interest in a subject still remains, which means guiding the students' thinking about a subject and challenging the student to be creative in his or her approach to analyzing the topic at hand. The teacher is a mentor and plays an interactive role with his or her students.

Internet resources allow science teachers to be highly creative in their teaching. For example, "An Ethernet-connected computer in the classroom allows for on-line demonstrations of weather systems" (Updegrove, 1995).

CRITERIA FOR EVALUATING MATERIALS

Web searching tools such as *Netscape, Mosaic,* and *Gopher* have made searching the Internet and publishing on the Internet very easy. Therefore, Web user sites are continually being added. Currently, there are at least 38 million people that are on-line (A Teacher's Guide to Understanding and Using the Internet, 1996).

There are more than 10 search engines. We found *Alta Vista, Excite, Magellan,* and *Yahoo!* to be the most important search engines for science education. For every hit with each search engine, there are over 5,000 sites on a given topic of research, making it impossible to go through all the sites. We usually went up to 40 sites and the categories and sub-categories for each of the sites that we visited. Although some sites sound very exciting, when you open them, the message is very disappointing: "File Not Found. . . . The requested URL was not found on this server." Most often, only one out of every 20 sites is "Net-worthy." Hence, searching is time consuming, often frustrating, and requires patience. How can teachers use the Internet meaningfully? How do we help our students select useful information? Mining for Internet-accessible resources is not that easy.

Following is a list of criteria for the selection of resources on the Internet:

1. The lesson plan on the Internet should match the goals and objectives of student learning.
2. Science content of an activity must be at the developmental level.
3. The reading level must be grade and age appropriate.
4. A Web site must present meaningful information and activities for both teachers and students.
5. Lesson plans and activities must reflect scientific inquiry, Science-Technology Society (STS), constructivism, integration, and multiapproaches to teaching and learning.
6. A Web site must have links to other related Web sites.
7. The Web site must have background information included with lesson plans.
8. The Web site must provide connections to experts, peers, teachers, or mailing lists.
9. Activities must be on-line or downloadable to local disks.
10. Information must have a multimedia approach—sound, movie, animation, and nice graphics presentations.
11. Articles and papers must have complete references.

We surfed through many Web sites in science education, and based on the above criteria, we have selected some sites that are useful for both teachers and students. For K–12 science you should surf through the Internet sites first and then recommend them to your students. This book actually has done part of this assignment for you.

The Internet can be incorporated easily into science teaching and learning. It offers both practical (providing information and activities) and theoretical (collaborating and construction) values and a shift in power from the teacher to the students.

CHAPTER SUMMARY

The Internet has now become the most sought-out on-line library. Science education becomes real and alive with the Internet. A virtual travel to the Smithsonian Institute will enable us to stop and explore the characteristics of many interesting gems and minerals. We should be able to use the Internet as well as help *our students* use the Internet. We as well as our students must learn "how to define what we are looking for, how to locate it, how to evaluate it, and how to use it effectively to communicate with others" (Morris, 1996). It has been projected that by the year 2000 every school in North America will be connected to the Internet. Teachers and students who do not use the Internet will be left behind in the stream of technology!

References

American Association for the Advancement of Science (1989). *Project 2061 Science for All Americans.* Washington, DC: National Academy Press.

Balliet, S. T. (1996). An Internet primer for teachers that have never worked with the Internet before. (http://members.tripod.com/~teachers/)

Friedman, E. A., Baron, J. D., & Addison, C. J. (1996). *Universal Access to Science.*

Hofstein, A. F., & Welch, W. W. (1984). The stability of attitudes towards science between junior and senior high school. *Research in Science and Technological Education, 2,* 124–138.

Jegede, O. J. (1989). Integrated science students' assessment of their teachers for characteristics of effective science teaching. *Research in Science and Technological Education, 7* (2), 235–247.

Kroeker, M. (1997). It's science fair time. *The Manitoba Science Teacher, 39* (2), 33–35.

Morris, J. L. (1996). *The technology revolution.* (http:///www.uvm.edu/~jmorris/comps2.html)

National Research Council (1996). *National Science Education Standards.* Washington, DC: National Academy Press.

O'Neil, J. (1995). Technology and schools: A conversation with Chris Dede. *Educational Leadership, October,* 7–12.

Study via Internet. *The Journal Technological Horizons in Education, 23* (11), 83–86.

Timmons, V., Liu, X., Macmillan, R., MacDonald, L., & MacKinnon, R. (1997). *Integration of Technology into Secondary Curriculum: Stage Two—Appendixes.* Antigonish, Nova Scotia: The Office of Learning Technologies, St. Francis Xavier University.

Updegrove, K. H. (1995). *Teaching on the Internet.* (http://pobox.upenn.edu/~kimu/teaching.html)

CHAPTER 3

Links to Science Activities

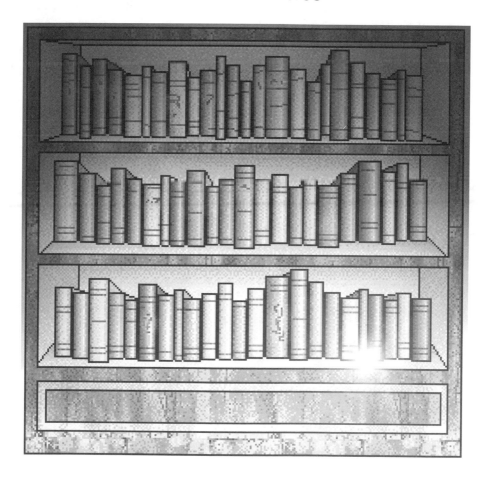

- Science Content Standards
- Earth and Space Science
- Life Science
- Physical Sciences
- General Science
- Elementary Science
- Secondary Science
- K–12 Science
- Science, Technology, and Society Connections
- Integrating Science and Other Curricular Areas

SCIENCE CONTENT STANDARDS

The American Association for the Advancement of Science (AAAS, 1989), the National Research Council (NRC, 1996), the Pan Canadian Curricular Frameworks (1997), and the Third International Mathematics and Science Study (TIMSS, 1994) outline recommendations for developing scientific literacy, "a more valid way to know how science works; a better sense of inquiry and its dependency on human need and discourse" (Ebenezer & Connor, 1998). In particular, the National Research Council outlines a set of science content standards and expects these to be a complete set of outcomes for students: "What students should know, understand, and be able to do in natural science" (NRC, 1996). These standards are:

- Science as inquiry
- Unifying concepts and processes in science
- Physical science
- Life science
- Earth and space science
- Science and technology
- Science in personal and social perspectives
- History and nature of science

Science concepts that are critical for every K–12 student are identified in Tables 3-1, 3-2, and 3-3 (National Research Council, 1996, pp. 109–111).

As you examine these content standards, consider how the Internet plays a role in developing scientific literacy. How does the Internet help "live out" the National Science Standards for teaching, learning, and assessment? Consider the Web sites in the following sections. The info-bar that will be used is shown below:

R	GL	TCK	RR	STS	IL	RTD

R	**Rating (* = Average, ** = Very Good)**	**STS**	**Science, Technology, and**
GL	**Grade Level**		**Society**
TCK	**Teacher Content Knowledge**	**IL**	**Inquiry Lessons**
RR	**Research Reports**	**RTD**	**Real-Time Data**

EARTH AND SPACE SCIENCE

An Astronomy Course for Middle/High School Students
URL:http://www.cnde.iastate.edu/staff/jtroeger/astronomy.html

This site provides an astronomy course for middle/high school students using the Internet. Information is well presented with key hyperlinks to more effective content areas. Topics available in this Web site include:

Table 3-1   Content Standards, Grades K–4

Unifying Concepts and Processes	Science as Inquiry	Physical Science	Life Science
Systems, order, and organization Evidence, models, and explanation Change, constancy, and measurement Evolution and equilibrium Form and function	Abilities necessary to do scientific inquiry Understandings about scientific inquiry	Properties of objects and materials Position and motion of objects Light, heat, electricity, and magnetism	Characteristics of organisms Life cycles of organisms Organisms and environments

Earth and Space Science	Science and Technology	Science in Personal and Social Perspectives	History and Nature of Science
Properties of earth materials Objects in the sky Changes in earth and sky	Abilities of technological design Understandings about science and technology Abilities to distinguish between natural objects and objects made by humans	Personal health Characteristics and changes in populations Types of resources Changes in environments Science and technology in local challenges	Science as a human endeavor

Reprinted with permission from the National Research Council (1996). *National Science Education Standards*. Washington, D.C.: National Academy Press.

- STARGZR, Sparkling Eyes, Happy Grins
- Observing the Night Sky
- Light Pollution
- Finding Your Way around the Sky
- Messages from the Cosmos
- Binoculars and Telescopes
- The Moon
- The Sun

Table 3-2:   Content Standards, Grades 5–8

Unifying Concepts and Processes	Science as Inquiry	Physical Science	Life Science
Systems, order, and organization Evidence, models, and explanation Change, constancy, and measurement Evolution and equilibrium Form and function	Abilities necessary to do scientific inquiry Understandings about scientific inquiry	Properties and changes of properties in matter Motions and forces Transfer of energy	Structure and function in living systems Reproduction and heredity Regulation and behavior Population and ecosystems Diversity and adaptations of organisms

Earth and Space Science	Science and Technology	Science in Personal and Social Perspectives	History and Nature of Science
Structure of the earth system Earth's history Earth in the solar system	Abilities of technological design Understandings about science and technology	Personal health Populations, resources, and environments Natural hazards Risks and benefits Science and technology in society	Science as a human endeavor Nature of science History of science

Reprinted with permission from the National Research Council (1996). *National Science Education Standards.* Washington, D.C.: National Academy Press.

■ The Solar System

■ Stars, Nebulae, and Star Clusters

■ Galaxies and Quasars

■ Cosmology

■ Other Really Cool Astrostuff

■ Who Writes This Stuff Anyway?

R	GL	TCK	RR	STS	IL	RTD
*	7–12	*				*

Table 3-3: Content Standards, Grades 9–12			
Unifying Concepts and Processes	**Science as Inquiry**	**Physical Science**	**Life Science**
Systems, order, and organization Evidence, models, and explanation Change, constancy, and measurement Evolution and equilibrium Form and function	Abilities necessary to do scientific inquiry Understandings about scientific inquiry	Structure of atoms Structure and properties of matter Chemical reactions Motions and forces Conservation of energy and increase in disorder Interactions of energy and matter	The cell Molecular basis of heredity Biological evolution Interdependence of organisms Matter, energy, and organization in living systems Behavior of organisms
Earth and Space Science	**Science and Technology**	**Science in Personal and Social Perspectives**	**History and Nature of Science**
Energy in the earth system Geochemical cycles Origin and evolution of the earth system Origin and evolution of the universe	Abilities of technological design Understandings about science and technology	Personal and community health Population growth Natural resources Environmental quality Natural and human-induced hazards Science and technology in local, national, and global challenges	Science as a human endeavor Nature of scientific knowledge Historical perspectives

Reprinted with permission from the National Research Council (1996). *National Science Education Standards.* Washington, D.C.: National Academy Press.

Athena Homepage
URL: http://athena.wednet.edu/

NASA and Science Applications International Cooperation (SAIC) feature a collection of on-line K–12 science lessons and instructional materials on oceans, earth resources, weather and atmosphere, and space and astronomy. For example, the lesson on hurricanes begins with journal writing, asking students to write what they know about hurricanes. The lessons consist of student activities and sheets, task cards, interdisciplinary projects, and further reading. The lessons have ample illustrations, and elementary school students will find it easy to read and follow the instructions.

R	GL	TCK	RR	STS	IL	RTD
**	K–12	*			*	*

Clouds Activities
URL: http://covis.atmos.uiuc.edu/guide/clouds/html/activities.html

This is a collection of illustrated lesson plans and activities on clouds for K–12 that encourages students to use journals to record observations, thoughts, and questions. Some lessons must be downloaded.

R	GL	TCK	RR	STS	IL	RTD
*	K–12			*	*	

Cool Science Resources
URL: http://www.teleport.com/~burrell/science.html

Jenna Burrell provides resource materials in astronomy, biology, chemistry, ecology, geology, meteorology, physics, and zoology. The subject matter provided in this site is very useful for students who are preparing for national examinations. For the teacher, Burrel provides in-depth background knowledge that will spur ideas for discussing science-related societal issues. Students will find this site very useful for research reports. This site also provides an e-mail facility to chat with experts in the field and links to other sites for both teachers and students.

Astronomy provides a virtual tour of the universe and includes information about each planet as well as many NASA expeditions. Stars and Galaxies has a multimedia approach to astronomy with movies and sound clips.

Chemistry provides an interactive table of elements and is very suitable for the preparation of AP and IB tests.

Ecology deals with science and the environment. There is a collection of articles about current environmental issues, and papers from the UN are available. This is an important site to visit if you are interested in issue-based teaching.

R	GL	TCK	RR	STS	IL	RTD
**	9–12	*	*	*		

Source: Curriculum Enhancement Consultants.

CurriculumWeb
**URL: http://www.curriculumweb.org/cw/ercntr/spiceislands/sivoyage/
       sivhome.html**

Spice Islands Voyage is an on-line distance learning adventure that offers activities
and resources in science among other curricular areas. Topics are: Rain forest, Volcanoes, Marine studies, Coral reefs, Manatees, and Spice Islands animals. Role-play
lesson plans and students' views about issues are presented.

R	GL	ICK	RR	STS	IL	RTD
**	4-8	*	*	*	*	*

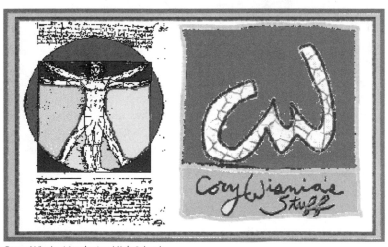

Source: Corey Wisnia, Mendocino High School.

Cory's World
URL: http://www.mcn.org/ed/CUR/cw/cwhome.html

Cory's World is a wizard's world that contains illustrative downloadable lessons
and units (including games) and other on-line science resources for the study of

astronomy and earth science in grades 3–8. This site includes listserv, projects, student-created stacks and Web pages, science poetry page, and kids' corner. The listservs are for science educators, and subscription will provide "updates on grants, curriculum, new or interesting science WWW sites, collaborative project updates from all over." This site is for students who can write and want to publish their own poetry about science-related topics, from nature observations to environmental topics to astronomy and earth science. Kids' Corner is "a place kids may wish to go to find neat sites for on-line interactive science!" You will read about a first-grade teacher who taught a thematic unit on birds. This teacher connected with 18 bird enthusiasts/experts around the USA and had her students send e-mail questions to them. A partial list of Science Education WWW URLs is available.

R	GL	TCK	RR	STS	IL	RTD
**	3–8	*	*	*	*	*

Reprinted with permission of Denver Earth Science Project.

Denver Earth Science Project
URL: http://www.mines.edu/Outreach/Cont_Ed/desp.shtml

The Denver Earth Science Project (DESP) is a K–12 curriculum development effort coordinated by the Colorado School of Mines. In partnership with corporations, federal agencies, school districts, and other institutions of higher education, a series of educational modules addressing a range of earth science topics has been developed:

1. Oil and Gas Exploration—grade level: 7–12

2. Ground Water Studies—grade level: 7–9

3. Paleontology and Dinosaurs—grade level: 7–1 0

4. Energy: A Closer Look at Oil and Gas—grade level: 4–6

5. Do You Know Your 3 Rs? Radiation, Radioactivity, and Radon—grade level: 7–10

These modules deal with critical issues facing society and are prepared by trained curriculum development teams composed of experienced earth science teachers and practicing scientists. The key to the success of the Project is the involvement of teachers in the design and writing of the materials. Each module is designed to incorporate input from teachers and industrial/governmental partners to assure technical accuracy and relevance to current situations." These modules may be obtained by writing to the URL.

R	GL	TCK	RR	STS	IL	RTD
*	7–12	*	*	*	*	*

Graphic used with permission of its creator, Chris Rowan.

Educational Space Simulations Project
URL: http://riceinfo.rice.edu/armadillo/Simulations/

This site is an outcome of the Educational Space Simulations Project sponsored by the Houston Independent School District and Rice University. "The purpose of this Web site is to promote the development of education via simulation. Although the primary focus of this site is space simulations, the concept of education via simulation is applicable to a wide range of disciplines."

This site provides resources and links to sites containing activities, lessons, and space simulations. Samples of student astronaut applications consist of an essay and an experimental proposal. You will see pictures of student-generated space simulation that show how to generate a weather report when participating in an educational space simulation.

This site is connected to other sites that are useful to space simulating educators. For example, this site is connected to educational materials available at Discovery Channel School and makes "links to articles, images, audio files, and animations regarding the discovery that life may have existed on Mars 3.6 billion years ago." Some of the important sites are:

WeatherNet

Space Shuttle Homepage

Microsoft Space Simulator

NASA Educational Workshop for Elementary School Teachers

NASA and Other Aerospace Centers

Quest's Online Interactive Projects

NASA's Spacelink

NASA's Shuttle-Mir Homepage

Yahoo! K–12 Sites

QUEST: NASA's K–12 Initiative

The Galileo Homepage

NASA Homepage

Spacelink Teacher Resource Center

The Institute for Space and Terrestrial Science

NASA Education

Planetariums on the Net

R	GL	TCK	RR	STS	IL	RTD
**	K–12	*	*	*	*	*

Homepage
URL: http://www.circles.org/

Curriculum. The Earth System Science Community (ESSC), consisting of educators, students, and scientists, provides an investigation-oriented earth system science curriculum. This curriculum enables high school and university students to research the earth system using earth observation data and information over the Internet.

Earth Science Data Services. The ESSC and the general public are using our data services to locate, visualize, and analyze earth science data in their research of the earth system.

Benefits of Science Understanding. Students and educators learn how to investigate the earth as a system using the appropriate scientific data, tools, and techniques.

Scientific Communications. Students also learn how to evaluate and publish the results of their team research on the Internet.

Knowledge Sharing. Scientists contribute their expertise, data, and research in the advancement of science education.

Broad Applicability. Because ESSC is inherently cross-disciplinary, the materials, tools, teaching resources, and examples of student research published on the ESSC Web sites may be used to supplement existing curricula in earth science.

R	GL	TCK	RR	STS	IL	RTD
*	9–12	*	*	*		*

Reprinted with permission of Hawaii Space Grant Consortium.

Exploring Planets in the Classroom: Hands-On Activities
URL: http://www.soest.hawaii.edu/SPACEGRANT/class_acts/

Hawaii Space Grant Consortium's Exploring Planets in the Classroom On-Line Activities was produced by scientists working with local teachers. This site provides more than 25 hands-on science activities in classroom-ready pages for both teachers and students for exploring geology, earth, the planets, and space sciences. These on-line activity pages are formatted for printing and direct classroom use. These resources are an outcome of annual summer courses in Planetary Geosciences offered at the University of Hawaii at Manoa for the state's K–12 teachers and librarians under the direction of Dr. G. Jeffrey Taylor. Hands-on activities in this course are developed and/or tested by the Hawaii Space Grant Consortium in cooperation with teachers statewide. Buttons on this site lead to activities such as:

Intro. to the Solar System

Planetary Properties

Volcanology

Impact Craters

The Dynamic Earth

Gradation

Gravity Forces and Rockets

The Moon

Remote Sensing

Planetary Science Research Discoveries' educational site is devoted to sharing the fascinating discoveries being made by NASA-sponsored planetary scientists. This site is a vital link for education, planetary research, and learning how science works.

This site connects to a National Science Teachers Association list of science and math links, NASA Space Link's electronic information system for educators.

R	GL	TCK	RR	STS	IL	RTD
*	6–12	*	*	*	*	

Frank Potter's Science Gems—Earth Science
URL: http://www-sci.lib.uci.edu/SEP/earth.html

Frank Potter categorizes more than 2,000 earth science links that are appropriate for your classroom and continues to add new resources weekly. Some popular sites are:

1. Measurement and Scientific Investigation
2. Our Earth in Space
3. Solar System
4. Astronomy
5. Atmosphere and Weather
6. Land and Geology
7. Oceans and Dynamics
8. Water and Its Effects
9. Resources—Energy, Minerals. . .

You will see:

■ Virtual Observatory on the Net
■ Views of the Solar System
■ Real-Time Satellite Earth Views
■ Space Shuttle Live!
■ Clickable World Maps
■ Weather Report Worldwide
■ Recent Earthquakes!!
■ Ocean Color Viewed from Space
■ Energy—Solar, Wind, etc.
■ Smithsonian Gems and Minerals
■ California Real-Time Traffic/Weather

This site offers resources for K–12 on the following subjects:

- Physical Science I
- Physical Science II
- Life Science
- Engineering
- Mathematics
- STS
- Health

For example, Kindergarten is the minimum level for Earth Science—Techniques: Measurement and Scientific Investigation.

There are K–12 lesson plans and background material on student reasoning or critical thinking by R. Paul. The minimum level is 3rd Grade.

This site includes Exploratorium Science Snackbook of Science Demonstrations—Exploratorium, San Francisco: a sample of about 20 "snacks" from the 100 in the book for simply constructing and investigating science, from optical illusions to electricity and light. Examples are colored shadows and hand battery.

In *Scientific Investigation* by L. Ginsberg and K. Essani, Western Michigan University: "Students are introduced here to the basis of scientific investigation. Making hypotheses and predictions, identifying components of experimental design, and data collection are performed in the lab. This Web page helps students with some common problems encountered with components of the experimental design, as well as how to present data (graphs and charts) and write a discussion."

Some of the other sites that this site is connected to are as follows:

The Franklin Institute Science Museum. There are: Virtual Exhibits (Ben Franklin—Glimpses of the Man; The Heart: A Virtual Exploration); educational hotlists; Lessons on Energy, Geology, Health, Space Science, Virtual Exhibits, Weather Science; and Virtual Exhibit Hotlist with links to many other exhibits and places. Examples include, Heart: Sizing Up; B. Franklin as a Scientist; and View of the Moon—Lorenzo in Italy.

Exploring Planets in the Classroom: Hands-on Activities from SpaceGrant Consortium at the University of Hawaii at Manoa. Dozens of lesson plans on the Solar System, Planets, Dynamic Earth, Volcanoes, Impact Craters, Moon, and Remote Sensing are included.

SeaWiFS Project Ocean Image Archive. G. C. Feldman at NASA. This site has pictures and temperature maps plus earth observation movies. Examples are Global Biosphere, Earth Observation Movies, and Sea Surface Temperatures.

In Amazonia from Space, you will find LANDSAT images used by PRODES (the Brazilian Amazon Deforestation Survey Project) in 1991. The minimum grade level is 9th Grade.

Newton's Apple Educational Materials. The site has more than 100 lessons and teacher guides for the 9th through 13th grades from brain mapping to bread chemistry to the Hubble telescope to printing money to a raptor hospital. Activities, questions, and further investigation suggestions are included. The minimum grade level is 6th Grade.

Lightning!! by P. J. Meyer and J. E. Arnold at NASA covers all you want to know about lightning including movies from the Space Shuttle missions, city lights at night from space, storm cells, and rainfall.

Current Weather in U.S. cities by P. Neilley at NCAR Weather has updates for hundreds of U.S. cities selected via maps or by text.

Weather by WedNet from NASA and SAIC includes lessons about hurricanes, clouds, weather charting, storms from space, precipitation, weather around the world, and some background material. Plenty of images and teacher discussion guides are available. The minimum level is 6th Grade.

Live from Antarctica—Passport to Knowledge Project Penguin contains images, hole in the ozone data, and links for teachers and students.

Smithsonian Gem and Mineral Collection. (photos by D. A. Penland) This site has about 100 marvelous pictures.

Family Science and Technology Activities frm Eduzone at Plymouth Public Schools has dozens of brief lesson plans for the family and their children to investigate plants and animals in their neighborhood, seeds and plants, the family tree, rocks, matter, light, and technology.

Virtual Antarctica includes TerraQuest maps, a virtual journey, pictures of the animals in the ocean around Antarctica, and a ship's log for the journey.

Virtual Fantastic Forest has National Geographic Maps, a virtual journey, and pictures of the animals and their habitats in the forest.

Electronic Gemstone Library from the Canadian Institute of Gemology: "[These] gemstones are the more popular ones usually set in jewelry found in retail stores."

Gemology and Lapidary. This site by J. F. Miller Multimedia (text and images) is a very large database on Gemology. Gemology and Lapidary includes the Rainbow of Gems (a list of gems); How are gems classified?; and How are gems cut and polished?

Acid Rain Resources from EcoNet (Select acid rain from the list.) includes numerous resource links for the waters of the seas, oceans, and rivers and links to acid rain research lessons.

Acid Rain Index to Resources by the Department of the Environment, Canada, has frequently asked questions about acid rain and numerous resource links.

Building a Solar House in Maine (CREST by W. Lord) is the continuing story of a new solar home—how it is being built and how it is working. Also, tables of solar radiation and climate data for comparison and calculation uses are included. Minimum level: 9th Grade.

Energy Resources. (CREST by C. Gronbeck) This site discusses energy resources from solar, wind power, small hydro, geothermal, and biomass and includes global impacts, economics, case studies, history, science concepts, and applications.

R	GL	TCK	RR	STS	IL	RTD
Best	K–12	*	*	*	*	*

Source: Jet Propulsion Lab, NASA.

Galileo K–12 Educator's Resources
URL: http://www.jpl.nasa.gov/galileo/educator.html

Galileo's Educational Outreach Office produces curriculum units, slide sets, and background sheets to add to your science lesson plans and to help your students keep up on current events when Galileo's mission is in the news. This promotes student's interest in solar system exploration. If you're a parent and your child's teacher doesn't have WWW access, you may consider downloading and printing out copies of any of the materials that you find here for use in your child's classroom. It also provides a layperson's explanation of the term *gravity assist.*

Online From Jupiter is for those who are interested in exploring the solar system or Jupiter and are curious about what it's like working behind the scenes on NASA's Galileo mission. You can peek over the shoulders of Galileo's scientists and engineers and read their responses to questions asked by K–12 students and teachers. Online also features classroom activities, journals, and more.

Music of the Spheres consists of songs contributed by the Galileo team to commemorate important mission events.

Teacher Contributions are some ways in which various teachers have utilized Galileo in their classrooms:

"Hey Kid, Want to Go to Jupiter?" (by Ron Rosano at rosano@well.com) gives your students a brief practical look at how to get a spacecraft to Jupiter. An explanation of gravity assists is suggested prior to doing the activity.

Page 1 (pdf file)

Page 2 (pdf file)

More links for educators are as follows:

Basics of Space Flight Tutorial is a higher-level overview of NASA Spacelink that includes tons of material and conferences for educators.

Welcome to the Planets, a pictorial tour of the solar system JPL Educational Outreach, is a comprehensive listing of NASA Education links.

Galileo Probe Educational Resources are educational briefs. The Observatorium, NASA's Remote Sensing Public Access Center, contains exhibits that help explain the mysteries of remote sensing in student-friendly terms. (See especially Learning Without Touching.)

Other Resources and Opportunities lists several non-Galileo-specific opportunities, resources, and programs that you may want to investigate.

Hardcopy versions of any educational resource may be obtained by contacting the Teaching Resource Center. The Galileo Resources Guide is a comprehensive listing of all Galileo educators' resources and how to obtain them. Integrating Galileo Resources into Your Classroom gives some ideas for classroom activities that use some of those resources.

R	GL	TCK	RR	STS	IL	RTD
**	6–12	*	*	*	*	*

GSFC Education K–8
URL: http://pao.gsfc.nasa.gov/gsfc/educ/k-12/K-8/K-8.htm

This includes a variety of K–8 lessons/activities for space and earth sciences from the Goddard Space Center. Examples of classroom lessons and activities are as follows:

- The first liquid fuel rocket and how it worked.
- Assemble your own Space Shuttle glider, a 1:200-scale model of the U.S. Space Shuttle orbiter.
- Scientific balloons
- Goddard missions of the 1990s
- Mission to Planet Earth (MTPE)—publications and education programs
- Earth science—on-line earth science education information forum
- Earth Observing System (EOS)—education
- TOMS Ozone—difference from climatology
- Total Ozone Mapping (TOMS)—homepage
- Earth view
- Living ocean—teachers' guide
- Global sea surface temperature
- First image of the global biosphere
- World cloud cover pattern

■ Tropical Rainfall Measuring Mission (TRMM)—science data and information system

■ Hubble Space Telescope first servicing mission

■ Astronauts training for Hubble Space Telescope servicing mission

■ Revealing secrets of the Big Bang

■ WIND laboratory

■ The exploration of the earth's magnetosphere

■ POLAR laboratory

■ Pegasus space launch vehicle

■ NASA's scout launch vehicle

■ The Delta expendable launch vehicle

■ Bright supernova captured in x-ray images

R	GL	TCK	RR	STS	IL	RTD
*	K–8	*	*	*	*	

Hands-on-Science
URL: http://dac3.pfrr.alaska.edu/~ddr/ASGP/HANDSON/

Hands-on-Science activities feature Ooze City: creating a complex city with microscopic inhabitants; Auroral Photography: capturing the aurora on the film; and Making Aurora: a classroom game. You will enjoy looking at this simple and yet interesting site.

R	GL	TCK	RR	STS	IL	RTD
*	K–8			*	*	

Reprinted with permission of Charles A. Wood, University of North Dakota.

Homepage of VolcanoWorld
URL: http://volcano.und.nodak.edu/

VolcanoWorld is supported by the NASA Program: Public Use of Earth and Space Science Data over the Internet. To find classroom lesson plans and activities, click on Learning about Volcanoes. For background information, click on Ask a Volcanologist, which features categories of answers to the most commonly asked questions about volcanoes. The site also includes a VolcanoWorld searcher where you can find lessons and other items.

R	GL	TCK	RR	STS	IL	RTD
**	4–12	*	*	*	*	*

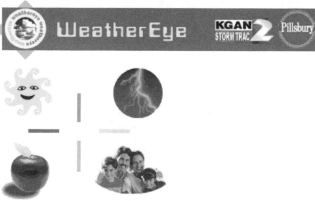

Reprinted with permission of Scott Hall, KGAN-TV.

KGAN WeatherEye Homepage
URL: http://weathereye.kgan.com/

Scott Hall and Roger Evans of KGAN Newschannel 2 in Cedar Rapids, Iowa, feature lesson plans and on-line resources for the study of weather in grades 2–12. The following resources are available:

- Cadet section for grades 2 to 8
- Expert section for grades 6 to 12
- Teachers' lounge lesson plans and resources
- Parents' center fun with your children!

R	GL	TCK	RR	STS	IL	RTD
**	2–12	*	*	*	*	

Source: Knowledge Adventure, Inc.

Knowledge Adventure Inc.
URL: http://www.adventure.com/

Knowledge Adventure considers learning to be serious fun. This site contains toddlers to age 2 science activities, space pictures, a scavenger hunt, and a reference library. Jump Start Elementary is a learning system that integrates the core components of elementary education. Find out about Knowledgeland, the new 3-D world. You can also play games, sample activities, and use a free reference library.

The following are some activities:

- Coloring fun with Casper awaits you in haunted Whipstaff Manor.
- Explore Knowledgeland.
- Play this month's *Java* game of the month!
- Don't miss the science lab, where whole new worlds come to life.
- Color in your favorite superhero in our movie theater.
- The library has a full encyclopedia, space pictures, and more!
- Check out Steven Spielberg's director's chair!
- Join the teachers' panel.

R	GL	TCK	RR	STS	IL	RTD
*	K–2	*		*		

Reprinted with permission of Northwest Regional Educational Laboratory, Portland, Oregon.

Library in the Sky
URL: http://www.nwrel.org/sky/

The Library in the Sky is for teachers, students, parents, librarians, and the community. It is sponsored by the Northwest Regional Educational Laboratory. Comprehensive educational resources, projects, discussions, collaborations, and standards for K–12 are available in various subject domains: arts, language, mathematics, science, social studies, health, and technology.

Science topics are as follows:

Astronomy

Biology

Botany

Chemistry

Earth sciences

Ecology

General science

Geography

Physics

Problem solving

Standards

Each science topic is generally organized into several sub-topics (e.g., biology—amphibians, birds, fish, insects, reptiles, and mammals), discussions with experts (e.g., ask an astronaut), lesson plans (e.g., global warming), lists (e.g., careers in biology), references and materials (e.g., construction plans for solar cookers), papers (e.g., understanding our planet through chemistry), periodicals (e.g., *Discover* magazine), projects (e.g., problem-solving activities in physics), and trips (e.g., Smithsonian gem and mineral collection).

R	GL	TCK	RR	STS	IL	RTD
**	K–12	*	*	*	*	*

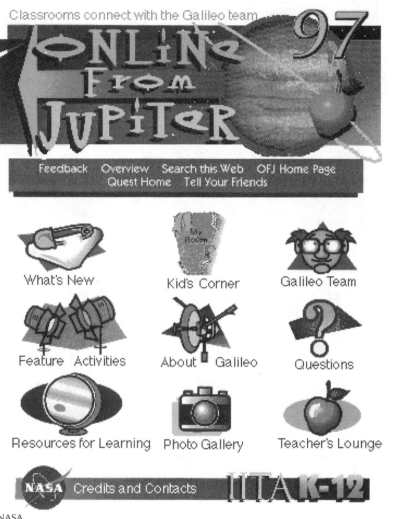

Source: NASA.

Online From Jupiter
URL: http://quest.arc.nasa.gov/project/jupiter.html

The Online From Jupiter project provides information about the Galileo mission to K–12 teachers.

Options include:

What's New with Online from Jupiter

Background about the spacecraft and its mission

Journal reports from Galileo personnel describing their day-to-day activities and their particular role in the project that will help students understand the diversity of people and skills that are needed for success in a modern science project

Biographical sketches of the men and women of the Galileo project that will help students relate to the project at a human level

An archive of previous Question/Answer pairs

Feature Activities meant especially to stimulate students

Resources for Learning, including curriculum materials about Jupiter and Galileo

A Teachers' Lounge that allows discussion among teachers (available through e-mail or the Internet) and includes a registration process that enables like-minded teachers to find one another for possible collaborations

A Photo Gallery of interesting and relevant images

R	GL	TCK	RR	STS	IL	RTD
*	K–12	*	*	*	*	

Science
URL: http://www.rsf.k12.ca.us/Subjects/Science.html

Science Oceanography Ocean Planet is a traveling exhibition. It features educational resources (lesson plans) as well as images and tours. Topics that are available include:

■ The lighthouse

■ Weather forecasts

■ The weather unit

■ Interactive weather browser

■ Current weather

■ Weather links

■ Forecasts

R	GL	TCK	RR	STS	IL	RTD
*	K–12	*	*	*	*	*

Source: NASA.

Spacelink Instructional Materials
URL: http://spacelink.msfc.nasa.gov/Instructional.Materials/.index.html

NASA provides a variety of downloadable interdisciplinary lesson plans, teacher activity guides, and video resource guides for learning about space for grades K–12. In addition, the site offers a wealth of curriculum materials and activities for the study of aeronautics, different topics in the sciences, and space technology tools. Topics are astronomy, chemistry, electronic resources for educators, environmental science, general science, geology, life sciences, microgravity, physical science, and physics.

R	GL	TCK	RR	STS	IL	RTD
*	K–12	*	*	*	*	

Source: NASA.

Space Science Curriculum Resources
URL: http://www.oise.on.ca/~mbegley/spaceweb.html

This Web site presents Internet resources in support of a science curriculum unit on the topic of space. These resources are intended for the junior to intermediate levels of elementary school science. Teachers should develop their own skill objectives, curriculum concepts, and learning outcomes based on the needs of their students. Integration of this science topic with language studies is possible through the science fiction section of this Web site.

Some information must be downloaded.

R	GL	TCK	RR	STS	IL	RTD
*	K–8	*	*	*	*	

MARS, SPECTRA, EARTHQUAKES, SINE WAVES, WHITE DWARFS, LIGHT

SATELLITES, VOLCANOES, CATACLYSMIC VARIABLE STARS, SIGNALS

Teacher-Developed Earth and Space Science Lessons and Classroom Activities

Reprinted with permission of the University of California, Berkeley.

Teacher-Developed Lesson Plans
URL: http://www.cea.berkeley.edu/Education/lessons/ lessons_teacherdeveloped.html

There are 16 teacher-developed earth and space science lessons that provide classroom demonstrations and activities for grades 4–12. Examples of lessons are solar system, earthquakes, and volcanoes, and there is a lesson template to create your own lesson. Students can conduct research through the Internet.

R	GL	TCK	RR	STS	IL	RTD
*	4–12	†	*	*	*	

Teacher Support Services
URL: http://www.aps.edu/htmlpages/tss.html

Elementary resources on earth and biological science include lesson plans and class activities for teachers and students. Some available links and resources include:

- Classroom activities
- Education staff at a glance
- Earth sciences resources
- Educational Native American network
- ERIC homepage
- Jurassic Park activities
- Kids visit the museum, 1995
- Mesa Elementary School in Albuquerque

R	GL	TCK	RR	STS	IL	RTD
**	K–6	*	*	*	*	

Source: Maura Hogan, U.S. Geological Survey.

Teaching in the Learning Web at the USGS
URL: http://www.usgs.gov/education/learnweb/

The U.S. Geological Survey provides earth science lessons for grades 1–12 that aim to increase scientific literacy. These lessons, tested and reviewed by teachers and students, meet the national earth science curriculum standards. Global Change features five classroom activities. Working with Maps includes an interdisciplinary set of materials on mapping for grades 7–12. Both topics include a teacher's guide, while the earth science topic offers pictures and activities about three faults. Other sites are included.

R	GL	TCK	RR	STS	IL	RTD
*	1–12	*	*	*	*	

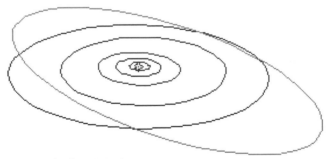

Reprinted with permission of William A. Arndt.

The Nine Planets
URL: http://seds.lpl.arizona.edu/nineplanets/nineplanets/nineplanets.html

The Nine Planets site provides detailed information about the solar system, graphically represented. Information includes an overview of the history, mythology, and current scientific knowledge of each of the planets and moons in our solar system. Each page has text and images while some have sounds and movies and most provide references to additional related information. This site is mainly for teacher content knowledge. Secondary students may use this site for doing research reports on planets.

R	GL	TCK	RR	STS	IL	RTD
**	K–12	*	*	*		*

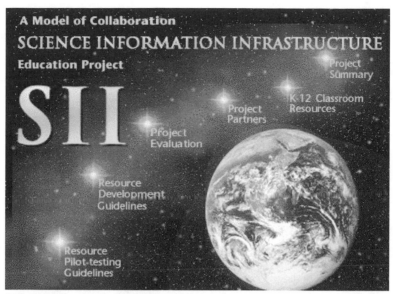

Source: © The University of California, Berkeley

The Science Information Infrastructure
URL: http://www.cea.berkeley.edu/Education/sii/sii_sii.html

This NASA-funded project has linked science museums, research centers, and teachers to produce earth and space science curricula for grades K–12 and public education. There is a teachers' page and a students' page. For example, Alan Goul provides an on-line activity for grades 4–12: "Is there 'ice' on Venus? If so, what KIND of 'ice' is it? In this activity, students will find the answers to these questions. This activity was inspired by a short news article in *Sky and Telescope* magazine about a rather unusual theory about 'ice' on Venus."

This site is linked to Teacher-Developed Lesson Plans.

R	GL	TCK	RR	STS	IL	RTD
**	K–12	*	*	*	*	

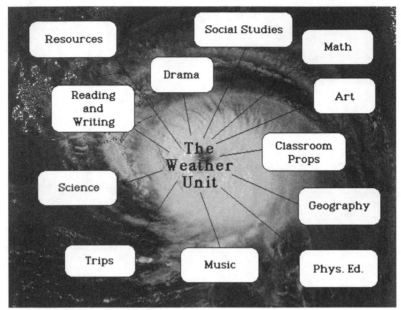

Source: William L. Chapman.

The Weather Unit
URL: http://faldo.atmos.uiuc.edu/WEATHER/weather.html

The Weather Unit develops a multidisciplinary approach. Science lesson plans related to weather for grades K–12 include precipitation, condensation, seasons, and evaporation. Teaching strategies include debate, story, experiment, and games.

R	GL	TCK	RR	STS	IL	RTD
*	K–12	*	*	*	*	

Source: Courtesy of Calvin J. Hamilton.

Views of the Solar System
URL: http://www.hawastsoc.org/solar

Views of the Solar System is an educational tour of the solar system. The table of contents has links to all of the site's various pages including lesson plans and activities. Views of the Solar System contains over 220 Web pages of information and over 950 pictures and animations of the sun, planets, moons, asteroids, comets, and meteoroids found within the solar system. The site also contains lesson activities.

R	GL	TCK	RR	STS	IL	RTD
**	4–12	*	*	*	*	*

Reprinted with permission of Chuck Wood, University of North Dakota.

Volcano Lesson Plans
URL: http://volcano.und.nodak.edu/vwdocs/vwlessons/lesson.html

VolcanoWorld provides students and teachers with hands-on lessons about volcanoes. The following materials are available:

1. A teacher's guide to the Geology of Hawaii Volcanoes National Park
2. UKESCC
3. Earth science lessons for grades 5–8
   Hyperstudio lessons
   On-line lessons
4. Mount St. Helens Living Lab Curriculum—lessons for grades 5–12
5. On-line lesson: Volcanoes by Lois Carter

R	GL	TCK	RR	STS	IL	RTD
*	5–12	*	*	*	*	

Source: Education Outreach Group.

Weather Here and There
URL: http://www.ncsa.uiuc.edu/edu/RSE/RSEred/WeatherHome.html

This is an integrated weather unit incorporating interactive, hands-on, collaborative problem-solving lessons and activities for students in grades 4–6. This unit is divided into 6 lessons. The lessons integrate math, science, geography, and language arts in the process of teaching and learning about weather phenomena. Students will become involved in collaborative problem-solving using e-mail as well as through joining projects offered via the Internet. The Global Education Project will help students see the relevance of science by interacting with scientists and other students across the world as they collaborate in the study of weather in their environment.

The first 3 lessons focus on learning basic meteorological concepts about weather elements, how to take measurements using appropriate weather instruments, and recognizing basic weather trends and patterns.

The last 3 lessons focus on studying weather maps and applying the knowledge and experience about weather to anticipate weather trends and patterns in the process of making accurate forecasts. The unit culminates with a weather broadcast of a 24-hour forecast presented by students and focusing on a network of weather stations in the US created by the students.

Unit directory

Unit objectives

Unit outline

Student pages

Lesson descriptions and objectives

Lesson I: characteristics of the earth's atmosphere

Lesson II: observing the weather

Lesson III: air affects weather

Lesson IV: plotting weather on the move

Lesson V: forecasting the weather

Lesson VI: broadcasting the weather
Suggested Internet sites
Illinois state science goals for learning
Bibliography

R	GL	TCK	RR	STS	IL	RTD
**	4–6	*	*	*	*	

Reprinted with permission of Corel Corporation.

Weather for Kids
URL: http://www.nwlink.com/~wxdude/kidres.html

This site provides teachers and parents with Nick's favorite resource materials for kids to learn more about weather and other sciences. "The Kids as Global Scientists Program is an Internet-enhanced curriculum designed to encourage middle school students in inquiry and research. Students use visualization and telecommunication technologies to learn about science both locally and through interactions with peers and resources worldwide." The students can also collaborate with scientists. This site is linked to The Weather Unit. Resource materials include:

- Musical meteorology from the Weather Dude (Audio)
- Nick's favorite weather books for kids
- Questions and quizzes
- Weather proverbs: nature's forecasters
- Free stuff by mail
- Meteorologist's tool box from the Weather Channel
- How to become a meteorologist
- Making a weather station
- Weather World from Penn State University
- Storm chasers homepage
- Storm photos
- Southeast Regional Climate Center weather and climate resources
- Earth and sky from the Radio Show

R	GL	TCK	RR	STS	IL	RTD
**	K–12	*	*	*	*	

Reprinted with permission of Sonya Cardenas, San Jose State University Foundation.

Welcome to STELLAR
URL: http://stellar.arc.nasa.gov/stellar/

Science Training for Enhancing Leadership and Learning through Accomplishments in Research (STELLAR), sponsored by the NASA Ames Research Center, features downloadable classroom activities and lesson plans developed by teachers for the study of space life sciences in grades K–12.

R	GL	TCK	RR	STS	IL	RTD
*	K–12	*	*	*	*	

Source: © University of Michigan and NASA.

Windows to the Universe
URL: http://windows.engin.umich.edu/

NASA has sponsored a dynamic presentation of earth and space sciences. Choose beginner, intermediate, or advanced interest levels.

R	GL	TCK	RR	STS	IL	RTD
*	6–12	*	*	*		

LIFE SCIENCE

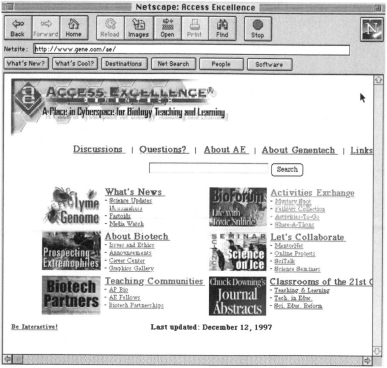

Source: Access Excellence and Genentech, Inc.

Access Excellence
URL: http://www.gene.com/ae/

This site consists of resources for biology teaching and learning. Resources include science updates, issues, and ethics about biotechnology, links to teaching communities, activities exchange, collaboration, and journal abstracts. High school biology teachers are connected with scientists, scientific information, and each other through the on-line network, Access Excellence. This national education program is sponsored by Genentech, Inc.

R	GL	TCK	RR	STS	IL	RTD
**	9–12	*	*	*		*

Source: The University of Arizona College of Agriculture.

Africanized Honey Bees on the Move Homepage
URL: http://ag.arizona.edu/AES/mac/ahb/ahbhome.html

Roberta Gibson at the University of Arizona features 30 lesson plans about honey bees and bee safety issues. These lessons are organized by grade clusters. The lesson plans are also integrated with information sheets that provide theoretical information for the teacher. Activity sheets are available for students.

R	GL	TCK	RR	STS	IL	RTD
**	K–12	*	*		*	

Reprinted with permission of Kathleen M. Fisher, San Diego State University.

Biology Lessons at SDSU
URL: http://www.biologylessons.sdsu.edu/index.html

Students at San Diego State University offer lesson plans in a variety of topics in biology for use in elementary school classrooms. This site presents lessons in molecules and cells and provides students and teachers with knowledge mapping and SemNet Web links to major biological content.

R	GL	TCK	RR	STS	IL	RTD
**	K–8				*	

Mini-Unit Topic: Insects
URL: http://www.ed.uiuc.edu/YLP94-95/Mini-units/Griffin.Insects/

A preservice teacher has prepared an introductory unit to the world of insects for grades 2 and 3. Suggested extension ideas are listed at the end of each lesson for those interested in developing this unit into an actual unit to be covered over an extended period of time (3 to 4 weeks). Some of the ideas for the art lesson are borrowed from the first 8-week cooperating teacher who taught an entire unit on insects. But most of the ideas for the other lessons are prepared by the preservice teacher. In addition to the 4 lessons required for this assignment, the preservice teacher has also made an entirely different lesson (partly based on one of the mini-unit lessons) for a 5th-grade class based on the second 8-week placement. This lesson may also be used in 2nd- or 3rd-grade classes, but the preservice teacher strongly suggests postponing the lesson until 4th or 5th grade due to its rather complex nature.

R	GL	TCK	RR	STS	IL	RTD
*	2–3					

SeaWiFS Project
URL: http://seawifs.gsfc.nasa.gov/SEAWIFS.html

NASA's Goddard Space Flight Center provides a teacher's guide featuring on-line activities with answers for high school students to study ocean color from space. The topics include life in the ocean, the ocean isn't just blue, phytoplankton, the earth, and carbon. Other resources include announcements, people collaboration, software documentation, technical reports, spacecraft information, receiving stations, mission operations, data sets images, and calibration validation.

R	GL	TCK	RR	STS	IL	RTD
*	11–12	*	*	*		*

The Yuckiest Site on the Internet
URL: http://www.yucky.com

The Yuckiest Site on the Internet features information about health, worms and cockroaches. To find a variety of resources, click on Your Gross & Cool Body, Wendell's Worm World, Ask Wendell, or Wendell's Yucky Bug World.

R	GL	TCK	RR	STS	IL	RTD
*	K–6	*				

Reprinted with permission of Kimberlye P. Joyce, University of Richmond.

Whales
URL: http://curry.edschool.Virginia.EDU/go/Whales/

Whales: A Thematic Web Unit is an integrated, interactive curriculum unit that can be used by teachers, students, and parents. The table of contents contains cooperative lesson plans (i.e., Teacher Guides from Sea World), teacher resources, interactive student activities, and projects with links to related sites.

R	GL	TCK	RR	STS	IL	RTD
**	4–8	*	*	*	*	*

Source: Wildlife Discovery Program and Houston Independent School District.

Wildlife Discovery
URL: http://www.rice.edu/armadillo/Schools/Hisdzoo/

The Houston Zoo and the Houston Independent School District present lessons for teaching about endangered animals for grades 3–6. Click on activity sheets that you can use at any zoo. The site also includes an on-line quiz about wild animals, a bilingual glossary of zoo terms, a list of frequently asked questions (FAQs), and facts about wildlife. Some of the information files must be downloaded.

R	GL	TCK	RR	STS	IL	RTD
**	3–6	*	*	*	*	*

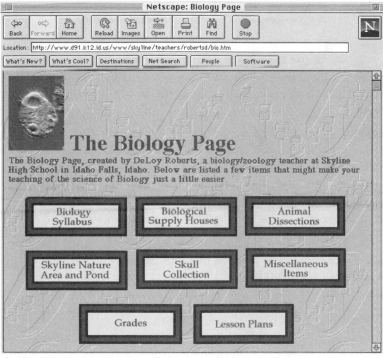

Reprinted with permission of DeLoy Roberts, Skyline High School.

The Biology Page
http://www.d91.k12.id.us/www/skyline/teachers/robertsd/bio.htm

The Biology Page is created by DeLoy Roberts, a biology/zoology teacher at Skyline High School in Idaho Falls, Idaho. He provides a syllabus for biology, dissections of animals, the collection of skulls, and a list of biological supply houses.

R	GL	TCK	RR	STS	IL	RTD
**	11–12	*	*	*		

Source: David Wighton, Community Learning Network.

Brain/Nervous System Theme Page
URL: http://www.etc.bc.ca/tdebhome/themes/brain.html

This site provides links to resources related to the study of the brain and nervous system. Students as well as teachers will find curricular resources and materials to help them learn about the brain and nervous system. Also, this site is linked to instructional materials (lesson plans) such as Neuroscience for Kids and Overview of the Brain.

R	GL	TCK	RR	STS	IL	RTD
**	K–12	*	*	*	*	*

Endangered Species Theme Page
URL: http://www.etc.bc.ca/tdebhome/themes/endangered.html

This site has links to information and content related to the study of endangered species. Lesson plans are also available for teachers and students. Interesting sites include For Kids Only: World Wildlife Fund Canada; Here Today, Gone Tomorrow?; and Investigating Endangered Species in the Classroom.

R	GL	TCK	RR	STS	IL	RTD
**	K–12	*	*	*	*	*

Photo reprinted with permission of Keith D. Turner, © 1996.

From the Ground Up
URL: http://www.gatewest.net/green/index.html

This site provides a teacher's guide that consists of lessons such as food, agriculture, and sustainable development: history of agriculture and description of sustainable development, soil, agriculture and chemicals, the real cost of food, and everything is connected. Lessons, background essays, and worksheets are available for downloading.

R	GL	TCK	RR	STS	IL	RTD
**	10–12	*	*	*	*	

Genetics/Biotechnology Theme Page
URL: http://www.etc.bc.ca/tdebhome/themes/genetics.html

This site has links to information and content related to the study of genetics and biotechnology. Lesson plans are also available for teachers and students. Interesting sites include Genetics Lesson Plan Ideas, Genetics and Public Issues, and DNA Learning Center.

R	GL	TCK	RR	STS	IL	RTD
**	10–12	*	*	*	*	*

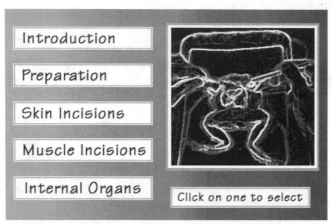

Reprinted with permission. Copyright 1994, Mable Kinzie.

Interactive Frog Dissection
URL: http://teach.virginia.edu/go/frog

This site teaches students how to dissect a frog and provides an understanding of the anatomy of frogs and vertebrate animals in general, including humans. Still and motion visuals of preserved frogs are shown.

R	GL	TCK	RR	STS	IL	RTD
**	10–12	*				*

Links. Fetal Pig Dissection Page
URL: http://hyperion.advanced.org/12014/links.html

This site provides numerous links to instruction materials on dissection. Sites include Science Kit's Homepage, the Dissection Lab, and Classification Lab.

R	GL	TCK	RR	STS	IL	RTD
**	10–12	*				*

Reprinted with permission of Southwest Educational Development Laboratory.

Integrating Mathematics, Science, and Language
URL: http://www.sedl.org/scimath/pasopartners

This site offers a series of multidisciplinary units. Each unit consists of an overview and background information for the teacher and lessons and links to associated Web sites. Units include: Kindergarten (Five Senses, Spiders, Dinosaurs); grade 1 (Plants and Seeds, the Human Body, Good Health); grade 2 (Oceans, Weather, Sun and Stars); grade 3 (Matter, Sound, Simple Machines).

R	GL	TCK	RR	STS	IL	RTD
**	K–3	*	*	*	*	*

Reprinted with permission of Janet W. Azbell, IBM Education, ISU.

Internet Activities
URL: http://www.solutions.ibm.com/k12/teacher/lp_text.html

In this site IBM provides a new set of Internet activities each month. Life science topics that have been developed include: Animals (grades 4–8); Gardening (grades 2–5); Forestry and trees (grades 5–8); Exploring insects and spiders (grades K–2, 3–5); and Zoo animals (grades 1–3). A teacher's guide is included for each topic.

R	GL	TCK	RR	STS	IL	RTD
**	K–8	*	*	*	*	*

Oceanography
URL: http://www.etc.bc.ca/tdebhome/themes/oceanography.html

This site has links to information and content related to the study of oceanography. Lesson plans are also available for teachers and students. Links such as the El Niño site, the Whales Theme Page, Elementary Lesson Plans, Resources on Oceans, Whales and Sea Life, and Sea World at Busch Gardens are available.

R	GL	TCK	RR	STS	IL	RTD
**	K–12	*	*	*	*	*

Respiratory System Theme Page
URL: http://www.etc.bc.ca/tdebhome/themes/respiratory.html

This site has links to the information and content related to the study of the respiratory system. Lesson plans are also available for teachers and students. Links such as the American Lung Association, Canadian Lung Association Resources, Grade 5 Life Science (Body Systems—Respiratory, Circulatory, Sensory), and Science Role Plays are available.

R	GL	TCK	RR	STS	IL	RTD
**	K–12	*	*	*	*	*

PHYSICAL SCIENCES

Source: Center for Polymer Studies, Boston University.

Center for Polymer Studies
URL: http://cps-www.bu.edu/

This scientific visualization research center develops experimental and computational materials for high school science education. Information resource links include Research Projects, Education Projects, Patterns in Nature Student Activity Guides, Fractals in Science Simulations (Java-Powered), the Dance of Chance Science Museum Exhibit, and Molecular Dynamics Simulations.

R	GL	TCK	RR	STS	IL	RTD
**	11–12	*	*			*

Umeå University
Analytical Chemistry

Reprinted with permission of Knut Irgum, Umeå University.

Chemistry Teaching Resources
URL: http://www.anachem.umu.se/eks/pointers.htm

Hundreds of chemistry resources are available for chemistry teachers, from lesson plans to reference guides to experiments. Sufficient resources are provided here for the chemistry teacher to toss out the textbook and use this site instead.

R	GL	TCK	RR	STS	IL	RTD
**	10–12	*	*	*	*	

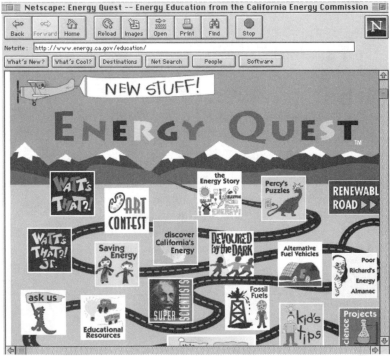

Reprinted with permission of the California Energy Commission.

Energy Quest Homepage
URL: http://www.energy.ca.gov/education/

This site contains activities and projects on alternative sources of energy, fuel vehicles, and energy safety.

R	GL	TCK	RR	STS	IL	RTD
*	K–12	*	*	*	*	

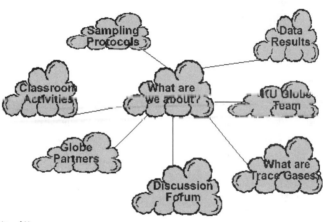

Source: University of Kansas.

KU's Trace Gas Project
URL: http://www.ukans.edu/~globe2/

K–12 students work with university scientists to collect and research ground-level trace gases. Included are lesson plans, classroom activities, student data collection, sampling protocols, discussion forums, and global collaboration.

R	GL	TCK	RR	STS	IL	RTD
*	K–12	*	*	*	*	

PEI Homepage
URL: http://www.pei.edu/

This site contains resources for teachers including lesson plans, interactive lessons, and chemical safety information. Many links are available.

R	GL	TCK	RR	STS	IL	RTD
**	K–12	*	*	*	*	*

Physical Science Lessons
**URL: http://www.eecs.umich.edu/mathscience/funexperiments/agesubject/
physicalsciences.html**

There are more than 100 physical science lessons for early elementary, later elementary, middle school, and high school students. Examples of lessons are:

- How do you make paper?
- How does soap work?
- The pizza box solar oven
- What is macaroni made of?
- What is thunder?
- Why does a steel nail sink while a steel boat floats?
- Playing with polymers
- Air bags and collisions: How do airbags prevent automobile injuries?
- Air pressure: What is air pressure, and how can it be measured?
- What makes the world turn around?
- Microwave ovens: What is the science behind microwave cooking?
- Slinky physics: How do toys work?
- What is infrared light, and how does it work?

R	GL	TCK	RR	STS	IL	RTD
**	K–12	*	*	*	*	

Source: Rick Wickling, Geometry Center, University of Minnesota.

Rainbow Lab
URL: http://www.geom.umn.edu/education/calc-init/rainbow/

This lab helps to answer these and other questions: How are rainbows formed? Why do they occur only when the sun is behind the observer? The outline for this site is as follows:

■ Objectives of the lab

■ How does light travel?

■ Reflection

■ Refraction

■ Rainbows: exploration

■ Rainbows: analysis

■ Conclusion

R	GL	TCK	RR	STS	IL	RTD
**	K–12	*	*	*	*	

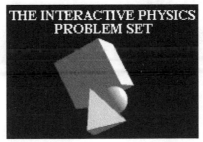

Source: © Regents of the University of California.

The Interactive Physics Problem Set
URL: http://info.itp.berkeley.edu/Vol1/Contents.html

The site consists of almost 100 practice problems for physics students with solutions and interactive experiments and Moving Pictures Experts Group (mpeg) movies.

R	GL	TCK	RR	STS	IL	RTD
*	11–12	*	*	*	*	

Reprinted with permission of Kyle Yamnitz, University of Missouri.

The Lesson Plans Page
URL: http://www.coe.missouri.edu/~kyle/edu.html

A teacher provides personal assignments and lesson plans on topics such as clouds and magnets. This page currently consists of links to lesson plan pages that are very helpful for anyone in education.

R	GL	TCK	RR	STS	IL	RTD
**	K–6	*	*	*	*	

Reprinted with permission of The Franklin Institute Science Museum.

Wind Our Fierce Friend
URL: http://sln.fi.edu/tfi/units/energy/wind.html

The Franklin Institute Museum of Science presents an interactive collaborative unit that investigates wind energy. The site contains lessons and activities that include student contributions from on-line schools. Content includes Blustery Beginnings, Investigating Wind Energy, Current Creations, and What Next?

R	GL	TCK	RR	STS	IL	RTD
*	4–6	*	*	*	*	

GENERAL SCIENCE

Activity Search
URL: http://www.hmco.com/hmco/school/search/activity2.html

Houghton Mifflin features a curriculum database where K-8 teachers can search for science lesson plans and activities by theme and grade level. Activities include Life Cycle of the Pacific Salmon, Catastrophe versus Accident—You Decide, Let's Make Waves, and Wind Direction.

R	GL	TCK	RR	STS	IL	RTD
*	K–8				*	

Source: W. J. Beaty.

Amateur Science
URL: http://www.eskimo.com/~billb/amasci.html

Amateur Science contains hundreds of science activities, experiments, and projects. Visit Bill Beaty's collection of science projects and the collection of science projects from various Web sites. Some of the sites include:

- Science Fair Stuff
- American Science Books
- Science Education Discussion Lists
- Science Education Stores
- Science and Surplus Suppliers
- Static Electricity Project Page
- Electronic Hobbyist Page
- Patents
- Bill B's Hobby Projects

R	GL	TCK	RR	STS	IL	RTD
**	4–12	*	*	*	*	*

General Science
URL: http://www.nwrel.org/sky/Classroom/Science/General_Science/
General_Science.html

General Science is a library in the sky for teachers, students, and parents. Main site headings available are Discussions, Lesson Plans, Lists, Materials, Multimedia, Papers, and Periodicals.

R	GL	TCK	RR	STS	IL	RTD
**	K–12	*	*	*	*	*

Source: KTCA TV, St. Paul, Minnesota.

Newton's Apple Index
URL: http://ericir.syr.edu/Projects/Newton/

Illustrated general science activities and lessons featured on TV are presented in this site. Lesson plans include Solar Powered Cars, Steroids, and Satellite Technology.

R	GL	TCK	RR	STS	IL	RTD
*	K–8	*	*	*	*	

Source: SAE International.

SAE's World in Motion Kit
URL: http://www.schoolnet.ca/worldinmotion

World in Motion, created by the Society of Automotive Engineers (SAE), provides five science units that will help you teach/learn about how people, objects, and everyday things move around in our world. Each unit contains a series of simple hands-on experiments that clarify the scientific principles.

R	GL	TCK	RR	STS	IL	RTD
*	4–8	*	*	*	*	

Science Lesson Plans
URL: gopher://bvsd.k12.co.us:70/11/Educational_Resources/Lesson_Plans/
    Big%20Sky/science

Gopher menu provides over 200 science lesson plans. Among its topics are color mixing, orbital paths, soil erosion, blood circulation, bird study, and crystals.

R	GL	TCK	RR	STS	IL	RTD
*	K–12	*	*	*	*	

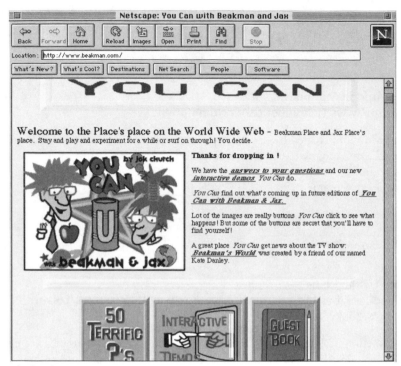

Source: Jok Church.

You Can with Beakman and Jax
URL: http://www.beakman.com/

Jok R. Church's television show *Beakman's World* can be used for science lessons. Click on 50 Terrific Questions, where you will find 39 questions and answers with accompanying science activities. Questions include: How does a lever make you stronger? Why do I hear weird sounds at night? How does yeast make bread rise? and What is thunder made out of?

R	GL	TCK	RR	STS	IL	RTD
**	K–8	*	*	*	*	*

ELEMENTARY SCIENCE

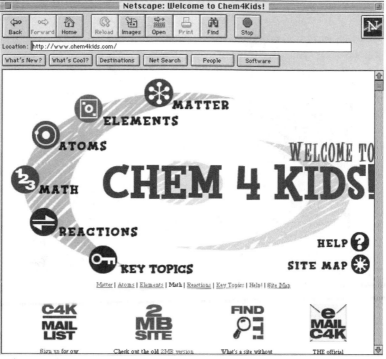

Source: Andrew S. Rader, Rader New Media

Chem 4 Kids
URL: http://www.chem4kids.com/

Chem 4 Kids teaches the basics of chemistry to children ages 5 to 11 in a fun way. The content outline includes matter, elements, atoms, and reactions.

R	GL	TCK	RR	STS	IL	RTD
*	K–8	*	*			

Reprinted with permission of the National Science Teachers Association.

Dragonfly
URL: http://www.muohio.edu/Dragonfly/index.htmlx

Dragonfly Web pages are for investigators of all ages. These pages go with *Dragonfly* magazine, but you do not need the magazine to have fun here. Right now the Dragonfly is exploring science and nature.

R	GL	TCK	RR	STS	IL	RTD
**	K–8	*	*	*		*

Source: University of Michigan.

Dr. Internet
URL: http://ipl.sils.umich.edu/youth/DrInternet/

Dr. Internet is for children to explore science fun and facts on the Web. The content outline for this site is as follows:

- Dr. Internet's Science Projects
- Explore the Internet with Dr. I.
- Science Fair Project Resource Guide

R	GL	TCK	RR	STS	IL	RTD
*	K–8	*	*	*	*	

Helping Your Child Learn Science
URL. http://www.ed.gov/pubs/parents/Science/index.html

This site has suggestions for parents to interest their children in science and includes basics about science and activities for children, including bubbles, plants, crystals, bugs, and soap powder.

R	GL	TCK	RR	STS	IL	RTD
*	K 8			*	*	

Highway to Science
URL: http://www.sd68.nanaimo.bc.ca/schools/coal/welcome.html

The Highway to Science Project Provides science lesson plans for elementary schools. This Web site contains science links in earth science, life science, and physical science.

R	GL	TCK	RR	STS	IL	RTD
**	K–8	*	*	*	*	

K–5 Curriculum Index
URL: http://groundhog.sprl.umich.edu/SEMCOG/K-5/

This index consists of science (STS-type) activities for air quality and smog and also the ozone layer. Some of the classroom activities provided in this Web site are:

1. Air is a gas: the properties of matter
2. Air can smell (and move)—with classroom map
3. How do living things use air?
4. Is all air clean?

R	GL	TCK	RR	STS	IL	RTD
*	K–5	*	*	*	*	

Science Activities Manual K–8
URL: http://www.utm.edu/departments/ed/cece/SAMK8.shtml

The Science Activities Manual (SAM) supports the K–8 Tennessee Science Curriculum Framework. SAM addresses content with a hands-on approach and also incorporates the skills necessary to raise the activity to a higher cognition level. This emphasis on both the physical and mental aspects of teaching and learning science is also called "touch science." The major motivation is to employ instructional strategies that bring the students *physically and mentally* into touch with the science they are studying.

R	GL	TCK	RR	STS	IL	RTD
*	K–8	*	*	*		*

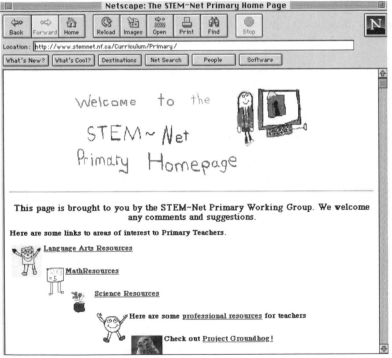

Source: Wendy M. King, STEM-Net Program Council.

STEM~Net Primary Homepage
URL: http://www.stemnet.nf.ca/Curriculum/Primary/

STEM~Net Primary Homepage provides a thematic unit on bears developed by preservice teachers from Memorial University in Newfoundland. It features a variety of cross-curricular lesson plans for students in the primary grades.

R	GL	TCK	RR	STS	IL	RTD

The Year Long Project 1996–1997
URL: http://www.ed.uiuc.edu/ylp/96-97/

University of Illinois at Champaign-Urbana and local elementary school teachers provide 11 cross-curricular science mini-units developed by student teachers and 8 cross-curricular science mini-units contributed by assistant teachers.

R	GL	TCK	RR	STS	IL	RTD
**	K–8	*	+	*	*	*

Reprinted with permission of Science Museum of Minnesota.

Thinking Fountain
URL: http://www.smm.org/sln/

The Science Museum of Minnesota provides an unusual collection of science activities on a site called the Thinking Fountain. An interactive graphic invites students, teachers, and other visitors to dive directly into the activities. The Thinking Fountain offers several additional ways to find an idea of interest, including going directly to an alphabetical listing, exploring by thematic topic, or typing in a word to search. Visitors to the site are encouraged to submit their own activities and questions to add to this wellspring of ideas.

R	GL	TCK	RR	STS	IL	RTD
**	K–6	*	*	*	*	

SECONDARY SCIENCE

Fun Science for Families Day
URL: http://pages.prodigy.com/LA/funscience/funscience.html

This is a clearing house for Fun Science information and demonstrates the fun and excitement of science. A few of the many sites listed on this Web site include Family Explorer, K–12 Science Education Resources, Exploratorium, and Science Daily.

R	GL	TCK	RR	STS	IL	RTD
**	K–12	*	*	*	*	*

Source: © 1995–1998 Katie Fliegler.

Homework Helper
URL: http://www.trabuco.org/

This site provides on-line homework help in all of the sciences. This Web site also provides a link to the NASA homepage.

R	GL	TCK	RR	STS	IL	RTD
**	K–12			*		

Inspire
URL: http://www.gsfc.nasa.gov/education/inspire/inspire_home.html

Inspire brings together high school students and other interested participants in the study of the earth's fascinating, naturally occurring radio signals (VLF).

R	GL	TCK	RR	STS	IL	RTD
*	11–12	*	*	*		*

Reprinted with permission of the National Science Teachers Association.

NSTA's Scope, Sequence, and Coordination Project
URL: http://www.gsh.org/NSTA

This is a science teacher journal for junior high students. It offers science educators and science enthusiasts hundreds of curricular resources and lesson plans.

R	GL	TCK	RR	STS	IL	RTD
**	9–12	*	*	*	*	

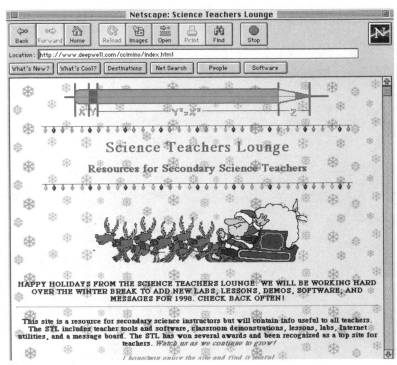

Source: Christoper Cimino.

Science Teachers Lounge
URL: http://www.deepwell.com/ccimino/index.html

This site provides resources for secondary science teachers including teacher tools
and educational software, classroom demonstrations, lessons, labs, Internet utilities, children's software, links to other cool science and education sites, and a message board.

R	GL	TCK	RR	STS	IL	RTD
**	9–12	*	*	*	*	*

UCSD Internet Lesson Plans
URL: http://ec.sdcs.k12.ca.us:70/11/lessons/UCSD_InternNet_Lessons

UCSD Internet Lesson Plans from the University of California at San Diego offers
a wide variety of science lessons and experiments covering biology, earth science,
physical science, chemistry, and physics for use in grades 7–12.

R	GL	TCK	RR	STS	IL	RTD
*	7–12			*	*	

K–12 SCIENCE

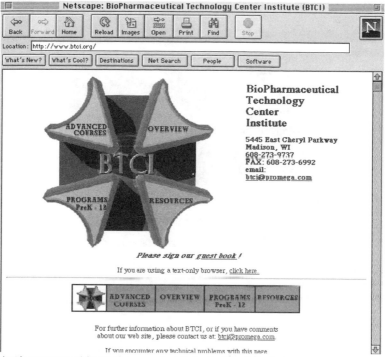

Reprinted with permission of the BioPharmaceutical Technology Center Institute.

BioPharmaceutical Technology Center Institute
URL: http://www.btci.org/

This site focuses on biotechnology training and education. Programs range from introductory lab activities for kindergartners to grade level courses for students, faculty, and industry scientists. A list of useful biotechnology resource books, articles, pamphlets, Web sites, and much more is included.

R	GL	TCK	RR	STS	IL	RTD
*	K–12	*	*	*		

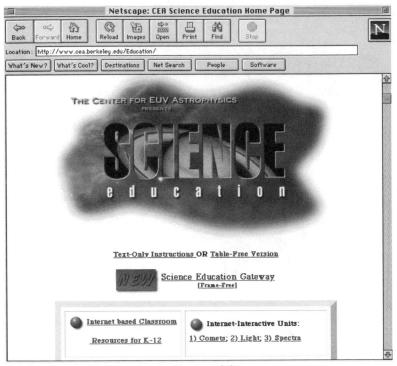

Reprinted with permission of the University of California, Berkeley.

CEA Science Education Home Page
URL: http://www.cea.berkeley.edu/Education/

This site contains Internet-Interactive Units on Comets, Light, and Spectra. Lesson plans and activities are designed by K–12 science teachers and students. Other subject indexes included in this Web site are Science Information Infrastructure (SII), Talk of the Town: A Discussion Forum Generator for Education, and the EUVE Slideshow.

R	GL	TCK	RR	STS	IL	RTD
**	K–12	*	*	*	*	*

Educational Hotlist
URL: http://sln.fi.edu/tfi/hotlists/hotlists.html

Educational Hotlist is divided into three main groups (general topics, science, and teacher resources) and includes lesson ideas and projects. Some of the topics include:

■ Atomic Structure
■ Chemistry 101

- Forensic Science Web site
- Einstein Revealed
- Chemical of the Week
- Chemicool—Periodic Table
- Complexity and Organic Development
- NIST Chemical Web book
- Electromagnetic Spectrum

R	GL	TCK	RR	STS	IL	RTD
**	K–12	*	*	*	*	*

General Links to Lesson Plans
URL: http://tikkun.ed.asu.edu/coe/links/lessons.html

For K-12.

Lesson Plans from ASKEric at Syracuse University (Gopher)

Elementary Science Lesson Plans (Gopher)

Holocaust Curriculum Plans (Gopher)

Lesson Plans in All Areas (Gopher)

Lesson Plans from ERIC-AE at Catholic University of America (Gopher)

Lesson Plans in Environmental Education (Gopher)

Lesson Plans in Science and Math from the HUB (Gopher)

Science Lesson Plans from Bolt, Beranek, and Newman (Gopher)

Lesson Plans from Teacher Talk Forum (WWW)

Lesson Plans and Projects from SAMI (WWW)

Lesson Plans and Resources for K–6 (WWW)

Classroom Resources for Environmental Education (WWW)

R	GL	TCK	RR	STS	IL	RTD
**	K–12	*	*	*	*	

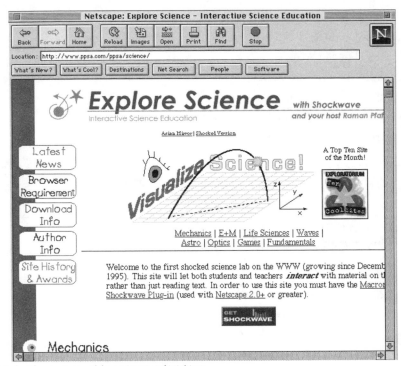

Reprinted with permission of the University of Michigan.

Interactive Science Education
URL: http://www.explorescience.com

Topics included are on-line experiments in mechanics, density, genetics, and plasma, including a frictionless inclined plane with sliding object. Other subject headings include Mechanics, E+M, Life Sciences, Waves, Astro, Optics, Games, and Fundamentals.

R	GL	TCK	RR	STS	IL	RTD
*	K–12	*	*	*	*	*

Internet School Library Media Center
URL: http://falcon.jmu.edu/~ramseyil/

This media center offers a comprehensive guide to children's and young adult literature, curriculum units, lesson plans, and resources in subject disciplines such as history, math, science, and social science.

R	GL	TCK	RR	STS	IL	RTD
*	K–12	*	*	*	*	

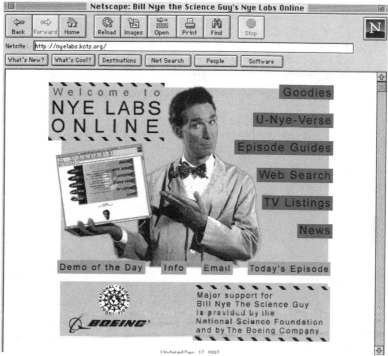

Source: Nye Labs Multimedia, KCTS Television.

Nye's Lab Online
URL: http://nyelabs.kcts.org/

Behind Bill's spinning head you will find his daily episode plus links to quality science education resources.

R	GL	TCK	RR	STS	IL	RTD
*	K–12	*	*	*		

Source: John Omar, GOALS (Global Online Adventure Learning Site).

Sailing thru Science
URL: http://www.goals.com/sailscin/sailscin.htm

It contains exercises and projects directly related to the scientific principles involved in circumnavigating the world. This site will help you understand global navigation, communication, and living at sea.

R	GL	TCK	RR	STS	IL	RTD
*	K–12	*	*	*		

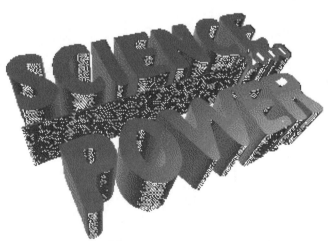

Source: Todd Hoover, Loyola University, Chicago.

Science Power
URL: http://www.luc.edu/schools/education/science.htm

Science Power has links to lesson plans and activities on natural science, earth science, astronomy and space, and Web sites. This is a great resource page for teachers.

R	GL	TCK	RR	STS	IL	RTD
**	K–12	*	*	*	*	*

Columbia University

Summer Science Research Program

Reprinted with permission of Jay Dubner, Columbia University.

Summer Research Program for Science Teachers
URL: http://cpmcnet.columbia.edu/dept/physio/

Summer Research Program for NYC Secondary School Science Teachers homepage contains laboratory research lesson plans developed by the participating teachers. Lesson plan topics include the Pressure-Volume Relationship in Gases (Boyle's Law), Vitamin C and protein analysis, and How is a tokamak used to produce controlled nuclear fusion?

R	GL	TCK	RR	STS	IL	RTD
**	K–12	*	*	*	*	

Teacher Tool Box
URL: http://www.trc.org/

Teacher Tool Box links to sites of interest to K–12 teachers and contains a searchable index where you can look for lesson plans or topics of your interest. There are quicklinks to several sites including MapQuest, Birdfoot's Grandpa, and Flea News.

R	GL	TCK	RR	STS	IL	RTD
**	K–12	*	*	*	*	*

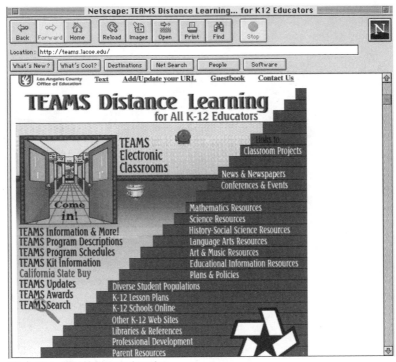

Source: Gayle Perry, TEAMS Distance Learning.

TEAMS Distance Learning—For K–12 Educators
URL: http://teams.lacoe.edu/

Telecommunication Education Advance for Mathematics and Science (TEAMS) distance learning, maintained by the Los Angeles County Office of Education (LACOE), features a variety of lessons, on-line classroom projects, and resources. Some of the interesting lesson plan sites listed are Air Quality Lesson Plans, Barbara's Lesson Plans in Science, and Biology Lessons for Prospective and Practicing Teachers.

R	GL	TCK	RR	STS	IL	RTD
**	K–12	*	*	*	*	*

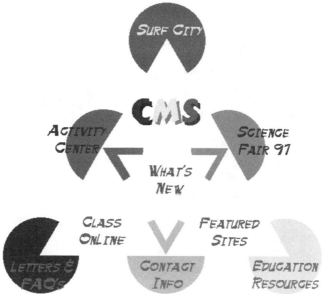

Source: Larry Dennis, Florida State University.

The Cyberspace Middle School
URL: http://www.scri.fsu.edu/~dennisl/CMS.html

This site is designed for students in the 6th, 7th, 8th, and 9th grades who are using the World Wide Web to assist their education and work on science fair projects. Menu headings in this site include Activity Center, Science Fair, Letters & FAQ's, Class Online, and Featured Sites. Some of the links available for science education are Understanding Our Planet through Chemistry, Rocketry Projects, and Exploratorium Home Page.

R	GL	TCK	RR	STS	IL	RTD
*	K–12	*	*	*	*	*

Reprinted with permission of Washington University School of Medicine.

The MAD Scientist Network
URL: http://128.252.223.239/~ysp/MSN/

The MAD Scientist Network—the laboratory that never sleeps—is a collective cranium of scientists from around the world fielding questions in different areas of science. Take a few moments to fill out the on-line question form if you need a question answered. You may also become a member of this Network. Subject headings include:

- *New* MadSci
- Circumnavigator
- Recently Answered Questions
- The MadSci Archives
- Search Our Site
- Ask a Question
- Check a Question's Status
- Join Our Efforts!

R	GL	TCK	RR	STS	IL	RTD
**	K–12	*	*	*		*

Whelmers Home Page
URL: http://www.mcrel.org/whelmers/

Activities on this site correspond with National Science Education standards. Some examples of activities are provided in this homepage. Information is provided in this site to order two volumes consisting of complete K–12 lesson plans. Some of the lesson plans available include Falling Test Tubes, Density Balloon, Energy Transfer, and Potato Float.

R	GL	TCK	RR	STS	IL	RTD
*	K–12	*	*	*	*	

SCIENCE, TECHNOLOGY, AND SOCIETY CONNECTIONS

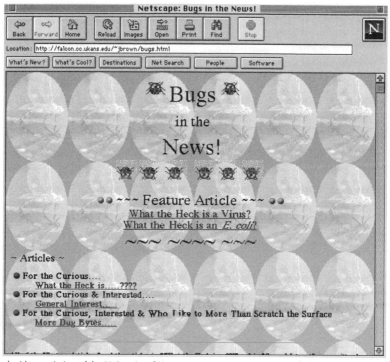

Reprinted with permission of the University of Kansas.

Bugs in the News
URL: http://falcon.cc.ukans.edu/~jbrown/bugs.html

A science professor offers scientific news and knowledge to information seekers in understandable, interesting language. As the title of the page implies, many of the science lessons here are inspired by yesterday's headlines. Two of the featured articles in this site are What the Heck is a Virus? and What the Heck is an *E. coli?*

R	GL	TCK	RR	STS	IL	RTD
*	9–12	*	*	*		

Events **Orbit**
Quiz **Quad**
Resource **Source**
Elementary **Planet**
Model **UN**
Curriculum **Corner**
Book Store
Guest **Book**

Source: CyberSchoolBus, produced by the United Nations.

CyberSchoolBus
URL: http://www.un.org/Pubs/CyberSchoolBus/

CyberSchoolBus, an interactive educational service, produced by the United Nations features lesson plans and activities on world issues, photos, competitions, and education resources. Some of the popular topics in this site include global trends, country at a glance, and a science puzzle.

R	GL	TCK	RR	STS	IL	RTD
*	K–12	*	*	*	*	*

Global Learning On-Line Homepage
URL: http://giraffe.rmplc.co.uk/eduweb/sites/rmext05/glo/

This site is for anyone interested in finding out or teaching about global issues. The site provides activities and information to get you thinking about global issues and to share good and bad experiences from using the Internet as a resource for global education, particularly in school.

R	GL	TCK	RR	STS	IL	RTD
*	K–12	*	*	*	*	

Keep America Beautiful, Inc.

Reprinted with permission of Keep America Beautiful.

Keep America Beautiful Homepage
URL: http://www.kab.org/

This site provides educational information on solid waste management (recycling, composting, waste-to-energy, sanitary landfilling) and litter prevention and offers free lesson plans and other publications on-line. Lesson plans available in this site include Waste: A Hidden Resource, Waste in Place, and Dirt Dessert!

R	GL	TCK	RR	STS	IL	RTD
*	K–12	*	*	*	*	

Liberty-Eylau's Teacher Lesson Plans Area
URL: http://198.38.64.1/lems/lessons.html

This site provides a variety of WWW links to Web sites that contain science lesson plans for teachers. Some of the sites listed include:

- ERIC Science Lessons
- Big Sky Science Lesson
- More Science Lessons from Doctor Sharp
- ERIC Technology Lessons
- Computer Skills Lesson Plans from North Carolina's Department of Public Instruction
- HTML Guides and Resources
- Teaching Computer Technology
- Investigating Endangered Species in the Classroom
- Programming by Ainsworth Lesson

R	GL	TCK	RR	STS	IL	RTD
**	K–12	*	*	*	*	

Reprinted with permission of Julie Chapin, National Network for Science & Technology.

National Network for Science & Technology
URL: http://www.uidaho.edu/ag/4-h/nnst/

This WWW site is for a youth development professional, a volunteer leader, or anyone looking for hands-on science and technology activities, science education research, or upcoming training and conferences. Resources fall within the scientific method and/or the exploratory learning model. Many of the resources will require adaptation to the nonformal setting.

R	GL	TCK	RR	STS	IL	RTD
**	K–12	*	*	*	*	*

National Science and Technology Week
URL: http://soundprint.brandywine.american.edu/~nstw/

This site houses information and activities to help you explore science and technology at school and at home. National Science and Technology Week was created by the National Science Foundation in 1984 to foster the public's understanding of and appreciation for the role that science and engineering play in everyone's life. Although efforts at enhancing the public's understanding and appreciation of these disciplines are year round, these efforts culminate annually in late April with National Science and Technology Week.

R	GL	TCK	RR	STS	IL	RTD
**	K–12	*	*	*	*	

NSTW '97—Teaching Activities
URL: http://www.nsf.gov/od/lpa/nstw/teach/start.htm

What's NSTW? How are bridges built over a body of water? Why is the sky blue? Why do ships float but rocks sink? What do earthworms eat? Where do stars come from? Will dinosaurs ever reappear? Is there life similar to earth's on other planets? These questions and thousands of others like them are from children who possess an endless sense of wonder about the world around them and how it works.

The National Science Foundation (NSF) believes that it is important to nurture the natural interests of children and the child in all of us about the wonders of science and technology. That's one of the reasons that more than a decade ago NSF started National Science and Technology Week (NSTW), celebrated at the end of April.

There are two broad components to NSTW: First, NSTW is a series of nationwide special events. The events range from family science nights to science and technology fairs to open houses to hands-on science and technology demonstrations sponsored by NSF and hundreds of community organizations, state agencies, museums, science centers, local businesses, national corporations, libraries, arboretums, planetariums, and zoos.

The second component is hands-on teaching activities that are developed and distributed free of charge to participating organizations. The materials are designed to stimulate both children's imaginations and their understanding of science and technology. By using these materials as instructional exercises, informal and formal science educators teach children how to observe real-world phenomena, analyze variables, draw conclusions, and evaluate findings.

Both the special events and teaching materials have one simple objective: heighten the awareness of children—and their parents and educators!—to the important role played by science and technology in everyday living.

R	GL	TCK	RR	STS	IL	RTD
**	K–12	*	*	*	*	**

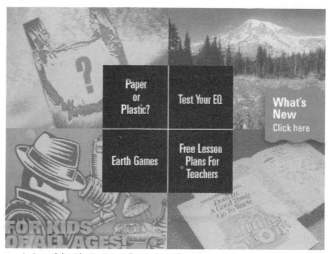

Reprinted with permission of the Plastic Bag Information Clearinghouse.

PBA Home Page
URL: http://www.plasticbag.com/

This site offers free environmental lesson plans for teachers on the 3 R's: reduce, reuse, and recycle. On-line activities for students dovetail with an activity poster. The lesson plans include Don't Let a Good Thing Go to Waste and An Ounce of Prevention.

R	GL	TCK	RR	STS	IL	RTD
**	K–12	*	*	*	*	*

Reduce, Reuse, Recycle, Revise, Respond
URL: http://www.ncsa.uiuc.edu/edu/classroom/k12-projects/summer/
recycle/index.html

Fisher Grade School's 5 Rs learning project is directed at improving grade 6 students' knowledge in environmental science and math as well as their attitudes and behaviors. Students are asked to explore questions related to the 5 Rs. Students examine: What is trash? How much trash do they produce as individuals? as families? as a school? How could they reduce the amount of trash they generate? What does their trash consist of? What does it mean to recycle? Does FGS have a recycling program? How could it be improved? What can they do to promote recycling at school? How does the village of Fisher dispose of its trash? How much trash do residents create? How does Fisher promote recycling? What are some concerns of the businesses and residents of the community?

R	GL	TCK	RR	STS	IL	RTD
*	6–12	*	*	*	*	*

The Living Curriculum Archive
URL: http://204.189.12.10/ed/cur/liv/ind/

The Archive contains lesson plans and unit descriptions with examples of student work in areas such as ecology, writing, math, and social science. Science topics include:

- Birds of a Feather by Jessica Morton, Mendocino Grammar School
- Flight: The Confluence of Dreams and Technology by Claire Skilton and Deena Zarlin, Mendocino Grammar School
- Science Mastery Units by Robert Miller, Mendocino High School
- Earthquakes by David Gross, Mendocino Middle School
- The Study of Local Ecology by Linda Leyva, Mendocino Middle School
- Salmon by Larry White, Mendocino Grammar School

R	GL	TCK	RR	STS	IL	RTD
*	K–12	*	*	*	*	

The Why Files
URL: http://whyfiles.news.wisc.edu/index.html

NSF sponsors an excellent weekly on-line magazine that addresses current science questions in the news. Recent articles include life on Mars and how tropical storms form. Available files in this site include Cloning, Migration, Climatology, Neutrinos, and Electric Cars.

R	GL	TCK	RR	STS	IL	RTD
**	8–12	*	*	*		*

INTEGRATING SCIENCE AND OTHER CURRICULAR AREAS

Birds: Our Environmental Indicators
URL: http://nceet.snre.umich.edu/Curriculum/toc.html

This is an entire curriculum plan from Earth Generation's New York Educator's Guide. Middle school students investigate birds as indicator species by learning about endangered species and environmental pollutants.

R	GL	TCK	RR	STS	IL	RTD
*	8–10	*	*	*	*	

Reading the Skies
URL: http://curry.edschool.Virginia.EDU/~tgl3e/skies/

Provides a framework for interdisciplinary instruction and accompanying lesson plans on astronomy and literature. The topic index includes:

■ Introduction—Van Gogh, Walt Whitman: How do humans use the stars?

■ Time—Hootie and the Blowfish, Shakespeare: archaeoastronomy

▥ Constellations—oral traditions: astronomy: fact and fiction

■ The Moon—"Two Leading Lights," the Dave Matthews Band: tidal charts

■ Our Solar System—*The Martian Chronicles,* "Fire and Ice"

■ Astronomers—Indigo Girls, historical links, and the *Spoon River Anthology*

■ Stars and Galaxies—Robert Frost: cosmology

■ Space Exploration and Colonization—Toad, Bradbury: colony design

■ Epilogue

R	GL	TCK	RR	STS	IL	RTD
*	6–12	*	*	*		

Reprinted courtesy of Smithsonian Office of Education.

SOE Home Page
URL: http://educate.si.edu/

Smithsonian Education provides on-line lesson plans from its quarterly magazine, *Smithsonian in Your Classroom,* integrating science and other curriculum areas. To find these plans, click on recent issues of *Smithsonian in Your Classroom.* More lesson plans from back issues are also available at this site. There are six interdisciplinary marine science lesson plans from the Smithsonian Ocean Planet exhibition. For more than 500 educational materials from the museum collection, click on Teachers Resources.

R	GL	TCK	RR	STS	IL	RTD
**	6–12	*	*	*	*	*

Teachnet.com: Lesson Ideas
URL: http://www.feist.com/~lshiney/lesson.html

Gradekeeper provides an alphabetized list of lesson plans and activities in science, health, and other subject areas. These lessons are designed by teachers for teachers. You may request a free e-mail newsletter featuring lesson plans and tips.

R	GL	TCK	RR	STS	IL	RTD
*	K–12	*	*	*	*	

Teacher Talk Forum

News & Info

Cyber Schools

Teacher References

Technology in the Classroom

Professional Development

References for Kids

Internet Fieldtrips

Lesson Plans

Museums

Reprinted with permission of the Center for Adolescent Studies.

Teacher Talk Forum
URL: http://education.indiana.edu/cas/ttforum/ttforum.html

The Center for Adolescent Studies at the Indiana University School of Education provides a collection of electronic lesson plans for science and health. Menu headings available at this site are: News, Lesson Plans, Professional Development Resources, Teacher References, Cyber Schools, Internet Fieldtrips, Museums, Technology in the Classroom, and References for Kids.

R	GL	TCK	RR	STS	IL	RTD
**	10–12	*	*	*	*	

CHAPTER SUMMARY

This chapter has provided you with many sites that will enable you to implement the National Science Education Standards. The sites identified in this chapter foster deeper understanding of science in its diverse domains. Just a click with the mouse at the sites provided in this chapter allows you to communicate with communities of scientists, science education researchers, teachers, and students. Science teachers and their students can actually have distant mentors answering their questions.

Reference

National Research Council (1996). *National Science Education Standards.* Washington, DC: National Academy Press.

CHAPTER 4

Science Curricular Frameworks

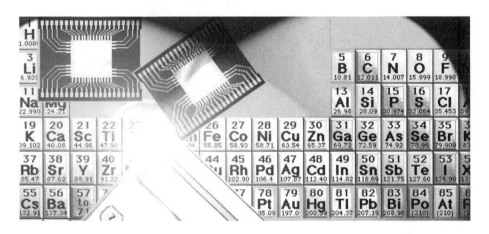

- Teaching and Learning
- Alternative Assessment
- Students' Conceptions
- History and Philosophy
- Ethics in Science and
  Scientific Issues

- Gender Equity
- Multicultural Science
- Informal Science
  Learning

The National Science Standards also include standards for science teaching, standards for professional development, standards for assessment in science education, standards for science education programs, and standards for science education systems (National Research Council, 1996, pp. 3–8). Hence, this book has included not only the Internet sites that pertain to the science content standards but also sites that will lead to the understanding of major topics and issues in science education:

Teaching and Learning
http://136.242.172.58/intass.htm

Assessment
http://www.cs.rice.edu:80/~mborrow/Lessons/assessls.html

Students' Alternate Conceptions
http://ascilite95.unimelb.edu.au/SMTU/ASCILITE95/abstracts/Akerlind.html

History and Philosophy
http://www.lhl.lib.mo.us/pubserv/hos/histsci.htm

Ethics in Science and Scientific Issues
http://www.cis.vt.edu/links/sts_links.html

Gender Equity
http://www.iptv.org/finelink/resources/fine_clean_summaries/
    38-gender.htm

Multicultural Science
http://www.inform.umd.edu:8080/UMS+State/UMD-Projects/MCTP/
    Technology/Minority.html

Informal Science Learning
http://www.lightlink.com/steve/

The following sections provide additional Web sites pertaining to curricular topics and issues in science education.

TEACHING AND LEARNING

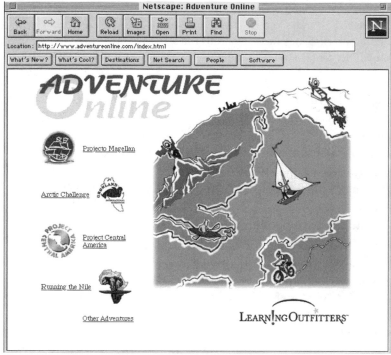

Reprinted with permission of Learning Outfitters, Inc.

Adventure Online
URL: http://www.adventureonline.com/index.html

Adventure Online teaching material can be used as an electronic textbook, media resource, language tutor, and map cabinet.

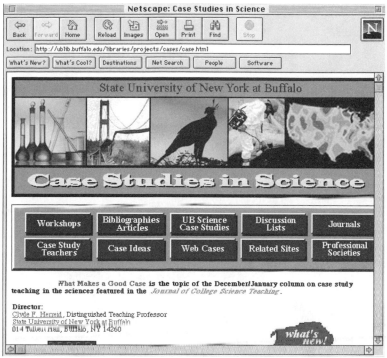

Reprinted with permission of UB Case Studies in Science Web Site.

Case Studies in Science
URL: http://ublib.buffalo.edu/libraries/projects/cases/case.html

The case method of teaching science is explored here. Resources are available for science teachers.

Classroom Material Homepage
URL: http://www.sonoma.edu/cthink/K12/k12class/trc.nclk

A wealth of information including instructional guides and lesson plans are provided in this site to help teachers implement critical thinking into every aspect of their teaching.

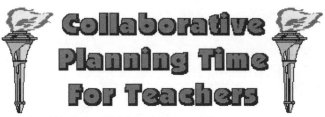

Reprinted with permission of Nottingham High School, Syracuse, NY.

Collaborative Planning Time For Teachers
URL : http://www.scsd.k12.ny.us/levy/colab.html

This Web page promotes as well as discusses the notion of collaborative work among teachers.

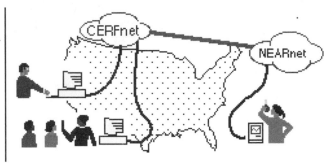

Source: Bill Borowy, Community of Explorers Lesson Plans, National Science Foundation.

Community of Explorers
URL: http://copernicus.bbn.com/WWW/CoE/coepage.html

The Community of Explorers involves the study of technology for building an electronic community of teachers and students. It explores new approaches to teaching high school science and provides students with inquiry environments for tackling fundamental concepts in physics and biology. Project researchers and teams of teachers in California and Massachusetts are investigating the use of computer modeling, data acquisition, and the Internet to help students understand science better. Using electronic mail, news, gopher, and World Wide Web capabilities, members communicate, collaborate, solve problems, and develop new learning materials.

Source: Andy Carvin, Corporation for Public Broadcasting.

EdWeb Exploring Technology and School Reform
URL: http://edweb.gsn.org/

Computers offer teachers a number of methods of enhancing successful teaching. There are so many different programs, networks, and computer-based lesson plans. Educators often struggle to decide which programs may be appropriate for a given subject or class. They must also consider questions of practicality, cost, and simplicity. To get a better understanding of how computers may be used in the classroom, take a look at some of the systems and services that educators have used to help their students learn and understand. These examples cover a range of methods, uses, and levels of sophistication, from complex to simple word processing and e-mail-driven lessons. Following each case are important issues for discussion.

Source: Creative Futures Project—Michael Schofield, Project Coordinator.

Creative Futures
URL: http://www.ozemail.com.au/~michaels/future.html

This project involves students joining classes around the world in a common classroom project via computers and the Internet. The program encourages children to write and draw about the future in society, science, and technology using the technology of the future. Classrooms are encouraged to share their work using the Internet.

Source: Cuisenaire.

Cuisenaire
URL: http://www.webcom.com/hardy/cuis2/activities.html

This site includes lesson plans and classroom activities in science. Submit ideas to the publishing group or the forum.

Source: Educational Online Sources, Providence, RI.

Educational Online Sources
URL: http://netspace.students.brown.edu/eos/main_image.html

Educational Online Sources is meant to be a first stop for educators exploring the Internet's potential as a teaching tool. This introductory page explains the EOS project and offers a link into the source list.

Educational Rendezvous
URL: http://www.ida.net/users/marie/ed.htm#SCIENCE

This page includes links to sites listed by subject and provides academic information.

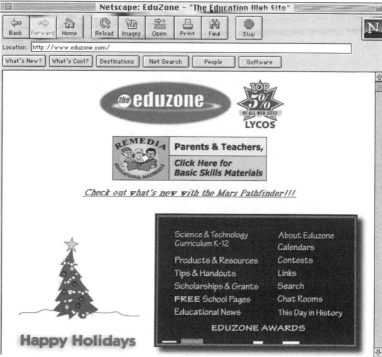

Source: ©Nybor Corp.

EduZone
URL: http://www.eduzone.com/

The EduZone provides teachers and educators a place on the Internet where all of their classroom preparation and professional development needs can be satisfied. Professional resources include a help wanted section, scholarship links, and suggestions for activities in the tips and handouts section.

Faculty Resource Center Homepage
URL: http://www.sonoma.edu/cthink/University/univclass/trc.nclk

Faculty Resource Center offers a wealth of information including instructional guides and lesson plans to help teachers implement critical thinking into every aspect of their teaching.

GC EduNET Lesson Plan Menu
URL: http://snow-white.gac.peachnet.edu/gather/LessonPlans/
lessonmenu.html

This site allows you to publish your own science lesson plans or browse what others have submitted.

Internet Connections
URL: http://www.mcrel.org/connect/

Internet Connections connects to a database of on-line education-related resources. Most have been created, maintained, and/or recommended by educators. New sites are being added continuously. Internet Connections is an education resource directory that includes topics such as assessment, family involvement, professional development, special education, and all subject areas. The lesson plans page is one of the most comprehensive on the Internet.

Reprinted with permission of Shelley Chamberlain, Lexington Public Schools.

Internet Exploration Guide for Teachers
URL: http://link.ci.lexington.ma.us/WWW/Shelley/homepage.html

This is a tutorial on the Internet that teaches you how to obtain teaching resources. This tutorial provides links as starting points to surf through the Internet to see what is available and what is beneficial to you.

Internet Starter Kit for Teachers
URL: http://home.earthlink.net:80/~agatt/

This site is designed to help elementary teachers who are new to the Internet. Some of the links will help you to find lesson plans, while others are useful if you are looking for educational sites for your students to visit.

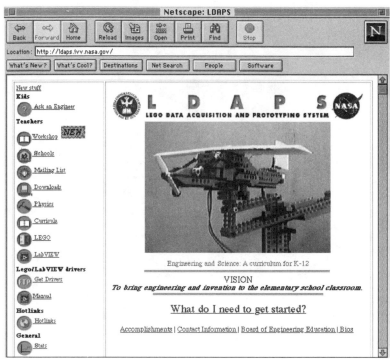

Source: Dr. Chris Rogers, Tufts University.

LDAPS
URL: http://ldaps.ivv.nasa.gov/

LDAPS develops and distributes materials to teach science through engineering and computers as an interdisciplinary methodology for teaching science.

Learning Studio
URL: http://www.exploratorium.edu/learning_studio/

Learning Studio is a multimedia and communications lab. It teaches you how to build classroom versions of Exploratorium exhibits and also includes a teacher's guide to student experiments.

Learning through Collaborative Visualization
URL: http://www.covis.nwu.edu/

This site supports teachers in transforming science learning to better resemble the authentic practice of science.

Lesson Plan Form
URL: http://cybershopping.com/eureka/lespln.html

Generate your own science lesson plan using Lesson Plan Form. You may submit your lesson plan on-line.

Let's Collaborate
URL: http://www.gene.com/ae/TSN/

Interact with scientists, teachers, and other classrooms to explore the cutting edge of science! Let's Collaborate connects biology teachers with leading researchers from around the country, linking the research-based community of scientists and science experts with the education-based community of teachers. Join Let's Collaborate for Science Seminars, SciTalk discussions, and Online Projects.

Reprinted with permission of Detroit Newspapers.

Newspapers in Education
URL: http://detnews.com/nie/

Newspapers in Education provides an extensive lesson plan archive for using public information sources in the classroom.

Possibilities in Science
URL: http://kendaco.telebyte.com/billband/Possibilities.html

Possibilities in Science integrates the Internet into the science classroom.

SAMI—Lesson Plans and Projects
URL: http://www.learner.org/content/k12/sami/lessons.shtml

SAMI provides extensive links to lesson plans and classroom ideas covering all study areas, including interactive WWW activities.

Source: Bill Brent.

Southwestern Bell Science Education Center
URL: http://tiger.coe.missouri.edu/~swbsc/

This center for K–12 science teachers helps them teach science and enhance the learning environment.

Teachers Helping Teachers
URL: http://www.pacificnet.net/~mandel/index.html

This is an IRC (Internet Relay Chat) site for teachers. Take the opportunity to chat with on-line teachers around the world.

Teachers Helping Teachers
URL: http://www.pacificnet.net/~mandel/Science.html

Teachers Helping Teachers, updated weekly, is a forum where teachers can share lesson plans/activities in science and other subject areas. The site also offers practical suggestions for classroom management.

Teaching with Electronic Technology
URL: http://www.wam.umd.edu/~mlhall/teaching.html

These sites pertain to using technology in the classroom.

The Computer Teacher's Resource Page
URL: http://nimbus.temple.edu:80/~jallis00/

This page is designed for the elementary school computer teacher who may be called upon to teach a computer class, maintain a computer lab, or provide guidance to other teachers. It provides Internet links to sites that can be used in creating classroom projects for every subject in the elementary curriculum. This page also offers links to educational research sites, Web design tools, and software resources.

KNOWLEDGE
INTEGRATION
ENVIRONMENT

Graduate School of Education
University of California at Berkeley
"Using the Net to foster a critical eye in science"

Source: Dr. Marcia Linn, University of California, Berkeley.

The KIE Curriculum
URL: http://www.kie.berkeley.edu/KIE/curriculum/curriculum.html

The KIE Curriculum involves students in projects in which they work with scientific evidence. KIE currently supports theory comparison, critique, and design projects. KIE can be used by science classes or for personal projects. When used in a classroom, KIE can complement other curricula such as laboratories.

Students using KIE reflect on their own scientific ideas while considering new evidence. Looking at information on the Net is necessary but not sufficient to complete a KIE project. Students must analyze evidence, producing scientific explanations for real-world phenomena. They learn how to create their own evidence related to a science topic and to design problem solutions based on scientific principles.

ALTERNATIVE ASSESSMENT

Assessments
URL: http://www.potsdam.edu:80/educ/glc/eisenhower/seeds/ assessments.html

This provides worksheets for student self-assessment. This form of assessment measures student understanding of the science concept, the science process skill being practiced, and the social skill being practiced. These worksheets become self-assessment tools when pupils are provided a chance to check their answers with one another and with a standard copy of the worksheet without the teacher providing input.

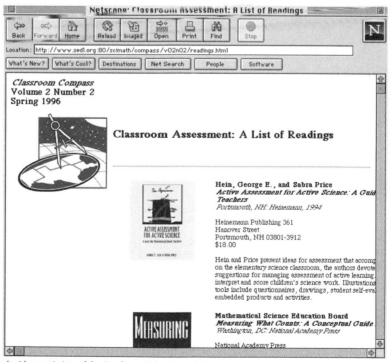

Reprinted with permission of the Southwest Educational Development Laboratory.

Classroom Assessment: A List of Readings
URL: http://www.sedl.org:80/scimath/compass/v02n02/readings.html

This issue of Classroom Compass gives a list of readings for classroom assessment (Austin, Tx: Southwest Educational Development Laboratory, 1996).

Martha's Alternative Assessment in Science
URL: http://www.cs.rice.edu:80/~mborrow/Lessons/assessls.html

Martha Borrowman provides a list of compilations of various sites she has found on the WWW that deal with using alternative assessment in science classrooms.

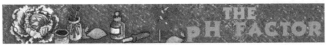

Reprinted with permission of the Miami Museum of Science, Inc.

Miami Museum of Science—Alternative Assessment
URL: http://www.miamisci.org:80/ph/lpexamine1.html

Addressed is the paradigm shift in education from the traditional teacher-directed classroom to a more active learning, student-based classroom. This shift creates the need for educators to re-evaluate the ways they have previously assessed student learning. It usually involves an extended, multistep production task, such as carrying out a project, or open-ended questions without a single correct answer, such as using alternative assessment to examine students' understanding about the pH factor.

Problem Solving Assessment
URL: http://www.enc.org/

These are resources and materials about problem-solving assessment.

SAIP '96 Science Assessment, CMEC
URL: http://ambra-168.cmec.ca/saip/scie96en.htm

This is a Canadian-based national science assessment.

Teacher TV—SAM's Tips & Links
URL: http://school.discovery.com:80/vvault/ttv/spring96/sams/wk18.html

This shows how students at Amanda Arnold Elementary School, Manhattan, Kansas, prepare and practice conference assessments to share with their parents in a meeting with the teacher. The Pathways to School Improvement Assessment Page offers information related to Rethinking Assessment and Its Role in Supporting Educational Reform, plus essays on Multidimensional Assessment.

STUDENTS' CONCEPTIONS

Students' Preconceptions of the Nature of Science
URL: http://www2.nas.edu:80/cuselib/27be.html

This site indicates the importance of becoming aware of students' preconceptions of natural phenomena and the improvement of science teaching in various subjects.

Mix or Match
URL: http://www.ed.ac.uk:80/~webscre/NL55Howe.html

This site discusses the usefulness of group work in science based on two conditions: that pupils have strong preconceptions about the topics being studied and that groups are given tasks that oblige them to make joint predictions based on their preconceptions, test the predictions against empirical data, and re-examine the preconceptions jointly in the light of the results.

Phenomenographic Research
URL: http://www.fit.qut.edu.au:80/InfoSys/bruce/anabib/e.html

This set of papers attempts to address complex issues of relational learning.

HISTORY AND PHILOSOPHY

Albert Einstein Online
URL: http://www.westegg.com/einstein/

On this site you can learn more about the life and theories of this century's most famous scientist. Selected writings and pictures are included.

Reprinted with permission of the Australian Science Archives Project.

ASAPWeb Homepage
URL:http://www.asap.unimelb.edu.au/

The Australian Science Archives Project, established in March 1985, locates, sorts, lists, and indexes the archival records of Australian scientists and scientific institutions. It provides documentary evidence of Australia's scientific past.

Reprinted with permission of the Tustin Unified School District.

Autumn Hall
URL: http://users.deltanet.com/~rblough/

Autumn Hall is the mythical place in the Scottish Highlands where young people studied to discover the scientific knowledge of the ages. Autumn Hall provides information and links to educational resources for the middle grade student and focuses on science.

Beginner's Guide to Research in the History of Science
URL: http://www.kaiwan.com/~lucknow/horus/guide/tp1.html

This site is an introduction to researching the history of science and includes a comprehensive listing of texts and publications.

Carmen Giunta's Classic Chemistry Page
URL: http://maple.lemoyne.edu/~giunta/index.html#historysites

The principal purpose of this site is to post the texts of several classic papers from the history of chemistry. This site also contains pointers to a few other chemistry-related sites and supports Carmen's courses. In early July, This Week in the History of Chemistry debuted and included links to sites about the listed person or events. Carmen intends to continue adding more classic papers. In addition, she will expand the texts of some papers that are currently listed as excerpts. If you like what you see, drop in again and see what's new. She welcomes comments and suggestions. Send e-mail to giunta@maple.lemoyne.edu.

18th Century History of Science Links
URL: http://www.english.upenn.edu/~jlynch/18th/science.html

Science and mathematics resources on the history of science are growing, but few focus specifically on the 18th century. Most of the sources provided are well organized, however, and will lead you to relevant material quickly.

Elementistory
URL: http://smallfry.dmu.ac.uk/chem/periodic/elementi.html

Investigate the history of each element in the periodic table from its discovery to the identification of its properties.

Evolution Entrance
URL: http://www.ucmp.berkeley.edu/history/evolution.html

This site outlines the contributions of major scientists between the 15th and 20th centuries in developing the theory of evolution.

Source: © 1997 University of Alabama. Tablet photo from University of Pennsylvania Museum, Philadelphia.

4,000 Years of Women in Science
URL: http://www.astr.ua.edu/4000WS/4000WS.html

This introductory guide to the role played by women in the history of science includes many short biographies and photographs.

GeoClio Homepage
URL: http://geoclio.st.usm.edu/

Details of meetings, projects, and discussion groups concerning the history of geology and the geosciences are provided.

History of Astronomy and Space Science
URL: http://wwwhpcc.astro.washington.edu/scied/astro/astrohistory.html

Links to articles on the birth of astronomy and space exploration, on-line exhibits, and descriptions of well-known observatories can be found here.

History of NASA
URL: http://www.gsfc.nasa.gov/hqpao/history.html

The development of NASA since 1915 with biographies of personnel, a space time-line, and histories of various installations are presented in this site.

History of Science Society Web Page
URL: http://weber.u.washington.edu/~hssexec/index.html

This is from a Seattle-based society dedicated to understanding science, technology, medicine, and their interactions with society over time.

History of Science, Technology, and Medicine
URL: http://www.asap.unimelb.edu.au/hstm/hstm_ove.htm

Enter a virtual library for many Internet resources on the history of science including biographies, magazines, and organizations.

Mendel Web Homepage
URL: http://www.netspace.org/MendelWeb/

This homepage provides a student guide that explores the influential experiments of Gregor Mendel and the origins of classical genetics.

Museum of Physics
URL: http://hpl33.na.infn.it/Museum-old/Museum.html

This site presents exhibits of early physics instruments at the University of Naples, including pictures and descriptions of use.

People of Astronomy
URL: http://bang.lanl.gov/solarsys/people.htm#Z

This is an a to z of scholars and details of all recipients of the Bruce Medal for life-time contribution to astronomy.

People Page
URL: http://www.teleport.com/~amobb/biology/people.html

Resources on scientists in genetics, including Darwin, Lamarck, Mendel, and Cuvier, and copies of their original papers are included.

Resources for Philosophy of Science
URL: http://www.ctr4process.org/resource/science.html

Resources for science and philosophy of science are provided.

The History of Chemical Engineering
URL: http://www.cems.umn.edu/~aiche_ug/history/h_intro.html

This investigates the history of chemical engineering and the growth of the industry over the last century.

The Nobel Foundation
URL: http://www.nobel.se/

The Foundation provides a searchable database of winners of the Nobel Prize for chemistry, physics, and medicine.

ETHICS IN SCIENCE AND SCIENTIFIC ISSUES

Biosis
URL: http://www.scicomm.org.uk/biosis/

Biosis gives you opportunities to ask questions and vote on issues such as the release of genetically modified organisms into the environment.

Source: Ethics Center for Engineering & Science.

Ethics Center
URL: http://ethics.cwru.edu/.

Resources for understanding and addressing ethically significant issues faced by scientists and engineers in their work are presented here.

Ethics in Science
URL: http://www.chem.vt.edu/ethics/ethics.html

Papers are available on ethics and scientific misconduct, with a bibliography of related publications and codes of professional conduct.

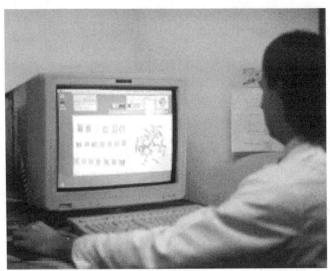

Reprinted with permission of the Swedish Medical Center, Seattle, WA.

Genetic Counseling
URL: http://www.gene.com/ae/AE/AEC/CC/counseling_background.html

Presented is an article on the history of counseling with information on coping with the human impact of genetic diseases.

Ifgene Index
URL: http://www.peak.org/~armstroj/

This is an organization aimed at encouraging the discussion of the moral and spiritual implications of genetic engineering.

On Being a Scientist
URL: http://www.nap.edu/readingroom/books/obas/

Presented is a National Academy of Sciences booklet on research ethics and responsible scientific conduct and a discussion of case studies.

Science and Ethics
**URL: http://www2.nap.edu/htbin/collection/exit=http%3A/
index%2Eopentext%2Enet/OTI%5FRobot%2Ehtml&colid=4%7C27**

Three documents are available on this site: On Being a Scientist: Responsible Conduct in Research; Women and Health Xenotransplantation; and Science, Ethics, and Public Policy.

Scientific Misconduct
URL: http://www.nyx.net/~wstewart/

This is a page full of resources and discussions on scientific misconduct.

Reprinted with permission of the University of Pennsylvania, Philadelphia, PA.

The Center for Bioethics
URL: http://www.med.upenn.edu/~bioethic/genetics.html

This University of Pennsylvania Center specializes in the implications of issues such as genetic engineering and medical malpractice.

Virtual STS
URL: http://helix.ucsd.edu/~bssimon/index.html

Professional organizations and projects for researchers in the fields of social and cultural studies of science are shown.

GENDER EQUITY

Access and Equity
URL: http://www.cew.wisc.edu/html_docs/access/access.html

This site promotes the idea that all students must have access to high-quality school-to-work programs and systems. All students, regardless of their economic, family, gender, or disability status, must have appropriate and personalized support services to successfully reach their educational and employment goals.

Source: NASA Ames Research Center.

Annotated Bibliography
URL: http://quest.arc.nasa.gov/women/resources/annbib.html

The site has instructional strategies to eliminate biases in learning resources and teaching.

Campbell-Kibler Associates, Inc.
URL: http://www.tiac.net/users/ckassoc/

User-friendly materials and resources for promoting gender equity in math and science in the coed classroom are provided.

Ensuring Equity and Excellence in Science
URL: http://www.ncrel.org/sdrs/areas/issues/content/cntareas/science/
      sc200.htm

Provided is a detailed discussion on ensuring equity. Equity has profound implications for teaching and learning science throughout the school community. The site suggests that ensuring equity and excellence must be at the core of systemic reform efforts not only in science but also in education as a whole. This site is full of useful information and links to help ensure gender equity in science.

Expect the Best from a Girl
URL: http://www.academic.org/

Lots of information about equity, tips for parents and educators, and links to other resources can be found.

Exploring Your Future in Math and Science
URL: http://www.cs.wisc.edu/~karavan/afl/home.html

The Women and Science page of the World Wide Web explores the reasons why women are less likely to enter professions in math and science and presents student opinions to let you know how beneficial it would be for society and the continuous advancement of women if more women were involved in the sciences.

4,000 Years of Women in Science
URL: http://crux.astr.ua.edu/4000WS/4000WS.html

This is a tremendous resource on women in science over the ages.

GAP On-line
URL: http://cml.rice.edu:80/~lanius/club/

Girls Are Powerful is a girls' technology council at Milby Science Institute, Houston, Texas.

Source: Province of British Columbia.

Gender Equity
URL: http://www.est.gov.bc.ca/curriculum/irps/music810/apcgen.htm

This is a summary of the preliminary "Report of the Gender Equity" by the Advisory Committee, British Columbia Ministry of Education, February 1994.

Gender Equity Publications
URL: http://www.newhorizons.org/equitypub.html

This is a source for many publications dealing with the issue of gender equity.

GENDER EQUITY   OPENING DOORS

Source: Special Programs Branch, British Columbia Ministry of Education.

Gender Equity Resource Catalog
URL: http://www.educ.gov.bc.ca/.gender/www/smandt.html

This site lists resources for achieving gender equity in science, math, and technology.

Gender Equity Science
URL: http://www.etc.bc.ca:80/apase/unmixed/unhome.html

Since there is not much material available on gender equity for classroom use and teachers take a considerable amount of time and effort to design their own material, this site provides gender-equitable science activities and resources. Included are activities that foster specific science skills such as deductive reasoning and invention through topics pertaining to elementary students' interests.

GirlTech
URL: http://www.crpc.rice.edu/CRPC/Women/GirlTECH/

This is a teacher training and student council sponsored by the Center for Research on Parallel Computing.

Promoting Gender and Social Equity
URL: http://www.educ.gov.bc.ca/.curriculum/www/irps/sciencek7/
    sciprom.htm

Instructional strategies to eliminate biases in learning resources and teaching are shown.

Research 2000
URL: http://www.aauw.org/2000/research.html

At this site you can find out about groundbreaking research conducted on the subject of gender equity in education.

TAP Junior
URL: http://www.cs.yale.edu/homes/tap/tap-junior.html

TAP Junior provides educational resources for encouraging girls and teens in science, computing, and technology.

Source: Yale Department of Computer Sciences.

The Ada Project
URL: http://www.cs.yale.edu/HTML/YALE/CS/HyPlans/tap/tap.html

This is a WWW site designed as a clearinghouse for information and resources relating to women in computing.

The AWSEM Project
URL: http://wwide.com/awsem.html

AWSEM's mission is to create and support a regional network of science and technology practitioners, educators, parents, businesses, and community organizations committed to the enrichment of opportunities in science, engineering, and mathematics for young women.

Source: The GEN © Commonwealth of Australia.

The Gen Homepage
URL: http://www.deet.gov.au/pubs/the_gen/

From Australia, this national newsletter offers an informal network for educators, students, parents, and others interested in gender issues in education.

Unmixed Messages
URL: http://www.etc.bc.ca/apase/unmixed/unhome.html

Strategies for Equitable Science Education: Unmixed Messages contains more than a dozen gender-equitable hands-on lesson plans for science in the elementary school. Included in the lesson plans are activities for chemistry with everyday materials, music exploring principles of sound, and science skills needed in deductive reasoning.

Women in Careers
URL: http://quest.arc.nasa.gov/women/POW.html

This is a K–12 Internet Initiative showing female role models in high-tech careers.

Source: Computer Science Dept., Keen University.

Women Into Science and Technology
URL: http://turbo.kean.edu/~wistproj/

The Women Into Science and Technology (WIST) project aims to attract and retain women in mathematics and science courses and careers through a multilevel activity and mentoring program. WIST involves and connects women at many stages: industry scientists, Kean College science faculty, Kean College science students, high school teachers, and high school students. Women act as mentors and mentees through a variety of activities. The project includes a network of female undergraduates, industrial scientists, and faculty members; a hands-on career awareness day at Kean College for 9th-grade girls; and ongoing mentoring and discussions at the high schools.

MULTICULTURAL SCIENCE

Source: American Indian Science and Engineering Society.

AISES Multicultural Education Reform Programs
URL: http://spot.colorado.edu/~aises/aises.html

This site provides a framework for learning about science, mathematics, and technology. By addressing each of these components, American Indian and other underrepresented minority students and their teachers can make meaningful cultural connections to teaching and learning. For additional information on specific programs, use the links provided at the bottom of the page.

Multicultural Science Education
URL: http://www.carleton.edu:81/curricular/EDUC/classes/educ338/
scied.html

This site provides information on the most effective changes in curricula involving efforts to show the limits of Western science and the contributions of people of all cultures while still maintaining a solid grounding in the dominant discourse of Western science. It also argues that curricula must also begin to teach that the technology and development that result from Western science have costs as well as benefits.

The Faces of Science
URL: http://www.lib.lsu.edu/lib/chem/display/faces.html

This site presents profiles of African Americans who have contributed to the advancement of science and engineering.

INFORMAL SCIENCE LEARNING

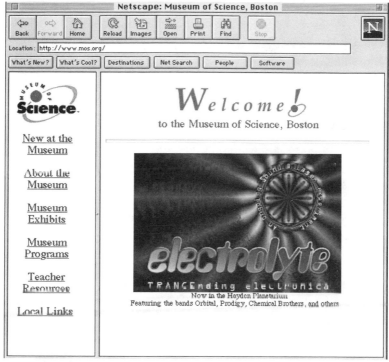

Source: Lance Lockwood, Boston Museum of Science.

Museum of Science, Boston
URL: http://www.mos.org/

Interactive exhibits featuring movies, photos, and resources for educators in the Science Learning Network are available.

Science Friday Kids Connection
URL: http://majorca.npr.org/sfkids/

Class activities and other support resources for NPR's weekly *Science Friday* radio show are shown.

Science Museums and Exhibits
URL: http://www-hpcc.astro.washington.edu/scied/
museum.html#scimuseum

This site presents extensive links to science museums and exhibits across the world.

Source: The Franklin Institute Science Museum.

The Franklin Institute Science Museum
URL: http://sln.fi.edu/tfi/welcome.html

The Franklin Institute Science Museum brings the exhibits, resources, and fun of a museum visit right to your desktop. The publications library provides *The Philadelphia Inquirer's Health & Science Magazine* as well as other science news, activities, and resources. The museum's units of study will support your science curriculum. Sample some interesting science programs and demonstrations.

Quite Amazing
URL: http://sln.fi.edu/qa96/amyindex.html

Amy investigates science and technology from a student's point of view at The Franklin Institute Online.

CHAPTER SUMMARY

This chapter highlights the curricular frameworks that the National Science Education Standards have outlined. The curricular frameworks include topics, trends, and issues. Prospective teachers, graduate students, and their mentors will find the sites in this chapter very useful in their courses.

Reference

National Research Council (1996). *National Science Education Standards.* Washington, DC: National Academy Press.

APPENDIX A

Professional Organizations

National Science Teachers Association

Reprinted with permission of NSTA.

NSTA
URL: http://www.nsta.org/

This site provides information about the National Science Teachers Association (NSTA). It is the largest organization in the world committed to promoting excellence and innovation in science teaching and learning for all. NSTA's current membership is more than 53,000. This includes science teachers, science supervisors, administrators, scientists, business and industry representatives, and others involved in science education.

NSTA addresses subjects of critical interest to science educators. The Association publishes five journals, a newspaper, many books, a new children's magazine called *Dragonfly,* and many other publications. NSTA conducts national and regional conventions that attract more than 30,000 attendees annually.

NSTA provides many programs and services for science educators including awards, professional development workshops, and educational tours. NSTA offers professional certification for science teachers in 8 teaching level and discipline area categories. In addition, NSTA has a World Wide Web site with links to state, national, and international science education organizations; an on-line catalog of publications; and two chat rooms to foster interaction and ongoing conversations about science education. NSTA's Web address is http://www.nsta.org.

NSTA's newest and largest initiative to date, Building a Presence for Science, seeks to improve science education and align science teaching to the National Science Education Standards nationwide. The Exxon Education Foundation has funded the initial effort to bring the program to 10 states and the District of Columbia.

The Association serves as an advocate for science educators by keeping its members and the general public informed about national issues and trends in science education. NSTA disseminates results from nationwide surveys and reports and offers testimony to Congress on science education–related legislation and other issues. The organization has position statements on issues such as teacher preparation, laboratory science, the use of animals in the classroom, laboratory safety, and elementary and middle level science.

NSTA is involved in cooperative working relationships with numerous educational organizations, government agencies, and private industries on a variety of projects.

NSTA
URL: http://www.nsta.org/pressrel/archive/spear.htm

This site provides information as to how NSTA (National Science Teacher Association) assists teachers to implement the National Science Education Standards in their classrooms. The book *A Framework for High School Science Education* shows how the content standards can be sequenced and integrated over 4 years of high school.

NSTA's Scope, Sequence & Coordination Project
URL: http://www.gsh.org/nsta_SSandC/

Scope, Sequence & Coordination is an NSTA project funded by the National Science Foundation. The project focuses on creating science programs at the secondary level based on the National Science Education Standards. This Web site offers several micro-units that are composed of labs, readings, and assessments for teachers and students.

Association for the Education of Teachers in Science
URL: http://science.cc.uwf.edu/aets/aets.html

This site provides information about the Association for the Education of Teachers in Science. It promotes leadership and provides support for those involved in the professional development of teachers. This includes teachers who:

■ Teach science education courses for prospective teachers
■ Provide in-service programs for elementary, middle level, or secondary teachers of science
■ Supervise, advise, or coordinate student teachers in science
■ Develop new approaches or materials for science teacher education
■ Conduct action research
■ Supervise graduate students in science education
■ Develop electronic media for use in science education

Source: American Association for the Advancement of Science.

The American Association for the Advancement of Science
URL: http://www.aaas.org/

This site provides information about the American Association for the Advancement of Science (AAAS, pronounced "Triple-A-S"), a nonprofit professional society dedicated to the advancement of scientific and technological excellence across all disciplines and to the public's understanding of science and technology. AAAS is among the oldest societies in America, having been founded in Philadelphia in 1848. Many of today's most prestigious and influential scientific societies have their historical origins in AAAS. For example, groups such as the American Chemical Society (1886), the American Anthropological Association (1902), and the Botanical Society of America (1906) all grew out of informal gatherings at AAAS annual meetings or from established AAAS Sections.

According to AAAS's Constitution, its mission is to:

Further the work of scientists

Facilitate cooperation among them

Foster scientific freedom and responsibility

Improve the effectiveness of science in the promotion of human welfare

Advance education in science

Increase the public's understanding and appreciation of the promise of scientific methods in human progress

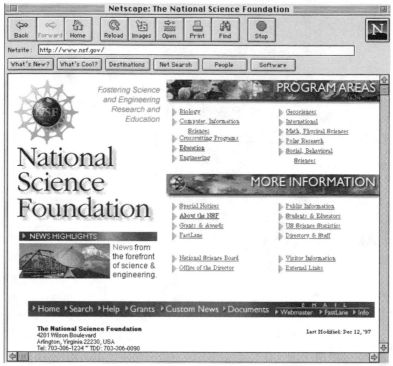

Source: National Science Foundation.

National Science Foundation
URL: http://www.nsf.gov/

This site provides information about the National Science Foundation. It is an independent U.S. government agency responsible for promoting science and engineering through programs that invest over $3.3 billion per year in almost 20,000 research and education projects in science and engineering.

Source: NASA

NASA Homepage
URL: http://www.nasa.gov/

This site is the homepage of NASA. NASA is committed to disseminate aeronautics and space research and provides education resources on the following strategic enterprises:

Aeronautics

Human Exploration and Development of Space

Mission to Planet Earth

Space Science

APPENDIX B

Financial Aid

Reprinted with permission of FinAid Page, Inc.

The Financial Aid Information Page
URL: http://www.finaid.org/

The Financial Aid Information Page provides a free comprehensive, independent, and objective guide to student financial aid. It is maintained by Mark Kantrowitz, author of *The Prentice Hall Guide to Scholarships and Fellowships for Math and Science Students,* and is sponsored by the National Association of Student Financial Aid Administrators (NASFAA).

APPENDIX

Electronic Journals

Breakthrough
URL: http://www.luciter.com/~sean/BT/

Breakthrough is a newsletter about important developments in science and technology.

Catalyst
URL: http://ted.educ.sfu.ca/catalyst/

This is British Columbia's homepage for teachers and students, particularly of biology, chemistry, geology, and physics.

Source: Cornell Science and Technology Magazine.

Cornell Science & Technology Magazine
URL: http://www.englib.cornell.edu/scitech/

This magazine is devoted to the coverage of new ideas, breakthroughs, controversies, and people in the worlds of science and engineering.

Reprinted with permission of Science Made Simple, Inc.

Science Made Simple
URL: http://www.waterw.com/~science/ck.html

This newsletter provides science help for parents and science fun for kids. It also gives answers to difficult science questions such as Why is the sky blue? Fun, safe, kid-tested projects are included. It will help provide answers for curious children. Each issue begins with a question children might ask as they notice the changing world around them. For example:

- Why is the sky blue? Why is the sunset red?
- Why are leaves green?
- Why do leaves change color in the fall?
- How do airplanes fly? How do boats float?
- Why don't spiders stick to their own webs?
- Why do people need glasses?
- How many meters are in a mile?

Source: CSIRO Publishing, Victoria, Australia.

CyberScience
URL: http://www.publish.csiro.au/cyberscience/

CSIRO, Australia's major scientific research organization, presents experiments, puzzles, magazines, and downloadable multimedia.

Discover Magazine
URL: http://www.enews.com/magazines/discover/

Complete on-line issues of the monthly general science journal are available free of charge.

Educator's Toolkit
URL: http://www.eagle.ca/~matink/

This site includes a monthly newsletter featuring reviews of educational Web sites, themes, lesson plans, and parent and teacher resources.

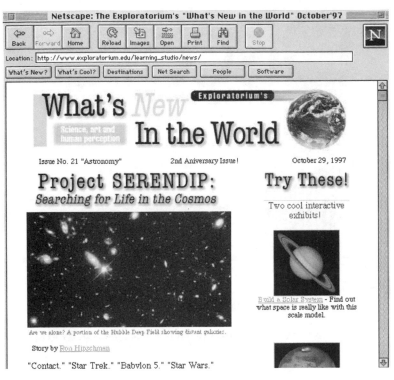

Reproduced with permission ©1998, Exploratorium, San Franciso.

Exploratorium's What's New in the World
URL: http://www.exploratorium.edu/learning_studio/news/

This is a monthly Internet publication that gives its readers concise information on the latest science news.

Reprinted with permission of La Recherche.

La Recherche
URL: http://weblarecherche.fr

This is a science magazine in French.

Reprinted with permission from *Nature*. Copyright Macmillan Magazines, Ltd.

International Weekly Journal of Science
URL: http://www.nature.com/

This is an international weekly journal of science.

ION Science
URL: http://www.injersey.com/Media/IonSci/

ION Science is "A fun site for science news—and one of the best." Included are news, features, and humor designed to make sense of science with weekly updates covering topics from dinosaurs to hurricanes to the latest in health and medicine.

University of California, Santa Cruz

Reprinted with permission of John Wilkes, University of California, Santa Cruz, CA.

Sciencenotes
URL: http://natsci.ucsc.edu/acad/scicom/SciNotes/BackIssues.html

Sciencenotes is a twice-a-year publication containing articles and essays by graduate students. It is written and illustrated by the students in the science communication program at the University of California, Santa Cruz. The Sciencenotes audience includes California high school teachers and students, UCSC alumni and campus community, and a small national audience of science writers and other interested readers.

Science and the Environment—A Learning Tool
URL: http://www.voyagepub.com/publish/voyage.htm

This electronic magazine brings you the most compelling environmental news from around the world. Articles are taken from over 500 magazines, specialized journals, and newspapers and are summarized in a concise format, complete with colorful photographs, maps, and graphics.

Source: © Scientific American.

Scientific American
URL: http://www.sciam.com/

The site provides enhanced versions of articles from the current issue, explorations of recent developments in the news, interviews, ask the experts, marketplace, and much more. Each issue contains 80 articles. Educational resources are designed for high school and university teachers (and students) who are looking for current news on the environment to supplement their texts and lesson plans.

Teacher Talk HomePage
URL: http://education.indiana.edu/cas/tt/tthmpg.html

An electronic publication for preservice and practicing secondary education teachers is presented here.

Reprinted with permission of John R. Heckman, Nebraska Wesleyan University.

The Empiricist
URL: http://biology.nebrwesleyan.edu/empiricist/

The Empiricist is an on-line journal dedicated to bringing the scientific method into high school classrooms. It is an active, research-based science curriculum that can inject excitement and promote the curiosity of high school students. The Empiricist provides an interactive, interesting, and peer-reviewed resource for teachers and students involved in high school research.

APPENDIX D

The Internet Language for Easy Surfing

The Internet has its own special language. An understanding of this language is an asset for easy surfing and communicating.

American Standard Code for Information Interchange (ASCII) is a format recognized by the computer as containing text and numbers and no graphics.

Archie is a software tool for locating files on FTP (File Transfer Protocol) sites. These sites are usually called anonymous FTP sites because a password is not necessary to log into the FTP site for downloading its resources. Log in as anonymous, and your password is your e-mail address.

Bandwidth, in bits per second, is a measure of how much data a modem transfers from one end to another. A fast modem in the 90s has the capacity to transfer or receive up to 30,000 bits per second.

Baud tells how many bits per second a modem can receive or send data. It is the measure of speed of the modem. Bandwidth is the measure of quantity. For example, a 2,400 baud modem transfers over 9,600 bits per sec of data.

Because It's There Network (BITNET) consists of educational sites networked together to form a group outside of the Internet. People in BITNET usually run under a Virtual Memory System (VMS), the main operating system used in mainframe machines. The BITNET is no longer popular.

Binary hexadecimal (Binhex) is a file that has been converted from a non-ASCII file to an ASCII file. This file is usually used for e-mailing because some e-mail software cannot read non-ASCII e-mail.

Bit is a number that the computer uses, either one or zero, to translate and understand data. It is the smallest unit of measurement in computer data.

Browser is software used on the Internet to view and extract resources from homepages and Web pages on the Internet. The popular browser programs are Netscape, Microsoft Internet Explorer, and Mosaic.

Bulletin Board System (BBS) is an on-line "get-together" system for people to share resources and ideas. A BBS system is hosted by an individual or a society. Check your local computer newspaper for the local BBS in your area.

Byte is made up of 8 bits. A kilobyte is about 1,024 bytes. A small diskette carries about 1.44 kilobytes.

Client is a software program designed to communicate and relay data from a server software program across one end to another. For example, in a computer network, one server computer controls two or more client computers.

Common Gateway Interface (CGI) is script-based software, usually written by programmers in Practical Extraction and Report Language (PERL), to instruct the Web server to carry out certain operations. CGI programs/scripts are usually put into a directory called cgi-bin.

Cyberspace, coined by William Gibson, describes the world of the Internet that carries a huge amount of informational resources through computer networks.

Domain, also known as DNS (Domain Name System), personalizes every computer in the world on the Internet. It gives a computer a number or word identification. www.altavista.com, for example, is a unique DNS. Nobody has the same DNS as another person.

Electronic-Mail (e-mail) is a software tool that is used on the Internet to send text across the Internet from one computer to another simultaneously.

File Transfer Protocol (FTP) is a method used to transfer files from one computer to another. You can use FTP with FTP software such as Fetch or Internet browsers.

Frequently Asked Questions (FAQs) is a place where people can look up answers to related questions on a particular subject of interest. You can get FAQs on the Internet through personal or commercial infobase Web pages.

Graphics Interchange Format (GIF) is graphic file formatted into GIF classification. Many of the Internet graphic files are in the GIF format. Another popular graphic format is jpg, which is a compressed graphic file.

Gopher is a traditional way to view and retrieve resources on the Internet. It is menu driven to help you find information resources quickly and efficiently. It has no graphic features. For Gopher servers you need Gopher Client software.

Homepage is an Internet site reached by an Internet browser. An Internet site starting with http:// protocol is called a homepage or a Web site.

Host is a computer that provides other computers on the computer networks or the Internet with a variety of services such as Gopher services, the WWW(World Wide Web), or just printing services.

Hypertext is text that can be linked to other documents by the click of a mouse. Hypertexts are underlined in blue.

HyperText Markup Language (HTML) refers to the computer scripting language. It is used to make Web pages or home pages. HTML documents can usually be recognized by their htm or html extensions such as guide2.html. HTML is used to format and lay out a Web page.

HyperText Transport Protocol (HTTP) is used on the Internet to locate hypertext information–based files. Sites with HTTP protocol means that they are World Wide Web sites.

Inter-Connected-Network (Internet) is a network of computers across the world that share informational resources. More than 50,000 computers are linked through the Internet to provide and share resource materials.

Internet Protocol Number (IP number) is a number used to identify your computer on the Internet. Your IP number on the Internet is your social insurance number.

Internet Relay Chat (IRC) is an on-line live chat environment on the Internet. IRC provides opportunities to communicate and conference with colleagues.

Internet Service Provider (ISP) is an organization that provides access to the Internet for a price.

Intranet is a private, local information–based network, the opposite of

Internet. No "outsider" can retrieve data from this network. The network resources are available only to members of the organization.

Listserv is a mailing list that belongs to a group of people with the same interest. Members can share ideas via e-mail.

Local Area Network is limited to a specific site or building.

Multipurpose Internet Mail Extensions (MIME) is used as a standard to include non-ASCII files with e-mail messages. Examples of non-ASCII files are sound, movie, and graphic files.

Newsgroup is a service provided for Internet discussions via e-mail. You can post messages on a "news" computer system. There are over 1,000 newsgroups.

Point-to-Point Protocol (PPP) enables a computer to initiate a normal connection (TCP/IP) through a modem and a telephone line to connect to the Internet.

Router is a computer hardware device used to connect two or more networks together.

Server is a computer or software package that initiates and relays all sorts of computer services to network client computers or client softwares.

Slip stands for the Serial Line Internet Protocol. It is similar to PPP.

Telnet is a communication command that connects one computer to another on the Internet. You can obtain any information from the host computer.

Uniform Resource Locator (URL) is the standard syntax to locate any resource available on the Internet. An example of a URL is http://home.cc. umanitoba.ca/

UNIX is a computer operating system for SUN computers. It is a multiuser operating system.

World Wide Web (WWW) is a system that enables you to browse through resource material on the Internet on-line. Gophers, FTP, and HTTP are all browsers on the WWW.